McDougal Littell
Algebra 1

Larson   Boswell   Kanold   Stiff

Notetaking Guide

The Notetaking Guide contains a lesson-by-lesson framework that allows students to take notes on and review the main concepts of each lesson in the textbook. Each Notetaking Guide lesson features worked-out examples and Checkpoint exercises. Each example has a number of write-on lines for students to complete, either in class as the example is discussed or at home as part of a review of the lesson. Each chapter concludes with a review of the main vocabulary of the chapter. Upon completion, each page of the Notetaking Guide can be used by students to help review for the test on that particular chapter.

McDougal Littell
A DIVISION OF HOUGHTON MIFFLIN COMPANY
Evanston, Illinois • Boston • Dallas

ISBN 13: 978-0-618-73691-1
ISBN 10: 0-618-73691-3

5 6 7 -CKI- 10 09 08 07

Contents
Algebra 1 Notetaking Guide

12 Rational Equations and Functions

13 Probability and Data Analysis

1.1 Evaluate Expressions

Goal • Evaluate algebraic expressions and use exponents.

Your Notes

VOCABULARY

Variable

> An algebraic expression is also called a variable expression.

Algebraic expression

Evaluating an expression

Power

Base

Exponent

ALGEBRAIC EXPRESSIONS

Algebraic Expression	Meaning	Operation
$7t$	7 times t	
$\dfrac{x}{20}$		Division
$y - 8$		
$12 + a$		

> To evaluate an expression, substitute a number for the variable, perform the operation(s), and simplify.

Example 1   *Evaluate algebraic expressions*

Evaluate the expression when $n = 4$.

a. $11 \times n = 11 \times$ ___   Substitute ___ for n.

    $=$ ___   _____.

b. $\dfrac{12}{n} = \dfrac{12}{\boxed{}}$ Substitute ___ for n.

    $=$ ___   _____.

c. $n - 3 =$ ___ $- 3$ Substitute ___ for n.

    $=$ ___   _____.

✔ *Checkpoint* **Evaluate the expression when $y = 8$.**

1. $7y$	2. $y \div 2$	3. $10 - y$	4. $y + 6$

Example 2   *Read and write powers*

Write the power in words and as a product.

Power	Words	Product
a. 12^1	twelve to the _____ power	_____
b. 2^3	two to the _____ power, or two _____	_____
c. $\left(\dfrac{1}{4}\right)^2$	one fourth to the _____ power, or one fourth _____	_____
d. a^4	a to the _____ power	_____

✔ **Checkpoint** Write the power in words and as a product.

5. 7^5	**6.** $\left(\dfrac{1}{3}\right)^2$	**7.** $(1.4)^3$

Example 3   *Evaluate powers*

Evaluate the expression.

a. y^3 when $y = 3$ **b.** a^5 when $a = 1.2$

Solution

a. $y^3 = $ ____^{3} Substitute ____ for y.

     $= $ _____   _____.

     $= $ _____   _____.

b. $a^5 = $ ____^{5} Substitute ____ for a.

     $= $ _____   _____.

     $= $ _____   _____.

✔ **Checkpoint** Evaluate the expression.

8. t^2 when $t = 3$	**9.** m^5 when $m = \dfrac{1}{2}$	**10.** x^3 when $x = 4$

Homework

1.2 Apply Order of Operations

Goal • Use the order of operations to evaluate expressions.

Your Notes

VOCABULARY

Order of Operations

ORDER OF OPERATIONS

To evaluate an expression involving more than one operation, use the following steps.

Step 1 Evaluate expressions inside _____

_____.

Step 2 Evaluate _____.

Step 3 _____ and divide from left to right.

Step 4 Add and _____ from left to right.

Example 1   *Evaluate Expressions*

Evaluate the expression $30 \times 2 \div 2^2 - 5$.

Solution

Step 1

There are no grouping symbols, so go to Step 2.

Step 2

$30 \times 2 \div 2^2 - 5 = 30 \times 2 \div \underline{} - 5$ _____

_____ **power.**

Step 3

$30 \times 2 \div \underline{} - 5 = \underline{} \div \underline{} - 5$ _____.

$\phantom{30 \times 2 \div \underline{xx} - 5} = \underline{} - 5$ _____.

Step 4

$\underline{} - 5 = \underline{}$ _____.

Your Notes

✔ *Checkpoint* **Evaluate the expression.**

1. $10 + 3^2$	**2.** $16 - 2^3 + 4$
3. $28 \div 2^2 + 1$	**4.** $4 \cdot 5^2 + 4$

Example 2 *Evaluate expressions with grouping symbols*

Evaluate the expression.

Grouping symbols such as parentheses ( ) and brackets [ ] indicate that operations inside the grouping symbols should be performed first.

a. $6(9 + 3) = 6(\underline{})$ 　　　　 _____ within parentheses.

$\quad\quad\quad\quad = \underline{}$ 　　　　 _____.

b. $50 - (3^2 + 1) = 50 - (\underline{} + 1)$ 　 _____ power.

$\quad\quad\quad\quad\quad\quad = 50 - (\underline{})$ 　 _____ within parentheses.

$\quad\quad\quad\quad\quad\quad = \underline{}$ 　　　　 _____.

c. $3[5 + (5^2 + 5)] = 3[5 + (\underline{} + 5)]$ 　 _____ power.

$\quad\quad\quad\quad\quad\quad = 3[5 + (\underline{})]$ 　 _____ within parentheses.

$\quad\quad\quad\quad\quad\quad = 3[\underline{}]$ 　　 _____ within brackets.

$\quad\quad\quad\quad\quad\quad = \underline{}$ 　　　　 _____.

✓ *Checkpoint* Evaluate the expression.

5. $6(3 + 3^2)$	6. $2[(10 - 4) \div 3]$

Example 3 *Evaluate an algebraic expression*

Evaluate the expression $\dfrac{12k}{3(k^2 + 4)}$ when $k = 2$.

Solution

> A fraction bar can act as a grouping symbol. Evaluate the numerator and denominator before dividing.

$$\dfrac{12k}{3(k^2 + 4)} = \dfrac{12(\boxed{})}{3(\boxed{}^2 + 4)}$$ Substitute ___ for k.

$$= \dfrac{12(\boxed{})}{3(\boxed{} + 4)}$$ _____ power.

$$= \dfrac{12(\boxed{})}{3(\boxed{})}$$ _____ within parentheses.

$$= \dfrac{\boxed{}}{\boxed{}}$$ _____ .

$$= \underline{}$$ _____ .

✓ *Checkpoint* Evaluate the expression when $x = 3$.

7. $x^3 - 5$	8. $\dfrac{6x + 2}{x + 7}$

1.3 Write Expressions

Goal • Translate verbal phrases into expressions.

VOCABULARY

Verbal model _____

_____

Rate _____

_____

Unit rate _____

TRANSLATING VERBAL PHRASES

Operation	Verbal Phrase	Expression
Addition	The _____ of 3 and a number n	_____
	A number x _____ 10	_____
Subtraction	The _____ of 7 and a number a	_____
	Twelve _____ than a number x	_____
Multiplication	Five _____ a number y	_____
	The _____ of 2 and a number n	_____
Division	The _____ of a number a and 6	_____
	Eight _____ into a number y	_____

Order is important when writing subtraction and division expressions.

> The words "the quantity" tell you what to group when translating verbal phrases.

Example 1 — Translate verbal phrases into expressions

Translate the verbal phrase into an expression.

Verbal Phrase	Expression
a. 6 less than the quantity 8 times a number *x*	_____
b. 2 times the sum of 5 and a number *a*	_____
c. The difference of 17 and the cube of a number *n*	_____

✔ *Checkpoint* **Translate the verbal phrase into an expression.**

1. The product of 5 and the quantity 12 plus a number *n*

_____

2. The quotient of 10 and the quantity a number *x* minus 3

Example 2 — Use a verbal model to write an expression

Food Drive You and three friends are collecting canned food for a food drive. You each collect the same number of cans. Write an expression for the total number of cans collected.

Solution

Step 1 Write a verbal model.   Amount × Number of
                                    of cans   _____

Step 2 Translate the verbal   ___ × ___
model into an
algebraic expression.

An expression that represents the total number of cans is _____.

✔ *Checkpoint* **Complete the following exercise.**

3. In Example 2, suppose that the total number of cans collected are distributed equally to 2 food banks. Write an expression that represents the number of cans each food bank receives.

Example 3   *Find a unit rate*

Three gallons of milk cost $9.15. Find the unit rate.

Solution

$$\frac{\boxed{}}{\boxed{}\ \text{gallons}} = \frac{\boxed{} \div 3}{\boxed{}\ \text{gallons} \div \boxed{}}$$

$$= \frac{\boxed{}}{\boxed{}\ \text{gallon}}$$

The unit rate is _____, or _____.

✔ *Checkpoint* **Find the unit rate.**

4. $\dfrac{420 \text{ miles}}{3 \text{ hours}}$	5. $\dfrac{\$12}{3 \text{ ft}^2}$	6. $\dfrac{20 \text{ cups}}{8 \text{ people}}$

Homework

1.4 Write Equations and Inequalities

Goal • Translate verbal sentences into equations or inequalities.

Your Notes

VOCABULARY

Open sentence

_____

Equation

_____

Inequality

_____

Solution of an equation

_____

Solution of an inequality

EXPRESSING OPEN SENTENCES

Symbol	Meaning	Associated Words
$a = b$	a is _____ to b	a is the _____ as b
$a < b$	a is _____ b	a is _____ than b
$a \leq b$	a is _____ than or _____ to b	a is _____ b, a is _____ than b
$a > b$	a is _____ b	a is _____ than b
$a \geq b$	a is _____ than or _____ to b	a is _____ b, a is _____ than b

---

Example 1 *Write equations and inequalities*

Write an equation or an inequality.

Verbal Sentence	Equation or Inequality
a. The sum of three times a number a and 4 is 25.	_____
b. The quotient of a number x and 4 is fewer than 10.	_____
c. A number n is greater than 6 and less than 12.	_____

> Sometimes two inequalities are combined. For example, the inequalities $a < b$ and $b < c$ can be combined to form the inequality $a < b < c$.

Example 2 *Check possible solutions*

Check whether 2 is a solution of the equation or inequality.

Equation or Inequality	Substitute	Conclusion
a. $7x - 8 = 9$	$7(2) - 8 \overset{?}{=} 9$	_____ _____ a solution.
b. $4 + 5y < 18$	$4 + 5(2) \overset{?}{<} 18$	_____ _____ a solution.
c. $6n - 9 \geq 2$	$6(2) - 9 \overset{?}{\geq} 2$	_____ _____ a solution.

✔ *Checkpoint* **Check whether the given number is a solution of the equation or inequality.**

1. $6r + 1 = 25$ $r = 4$	**2.** $x^2 - 5 > 10$ $x = 5$	**3.** $7a \leq 21$ $a = 6$

Example 3 *Use mental math to solve an equation*

Solve the equation using mental math.

a. $n + 6 = 11$ 　　　　　　　　**b.** $18 - x = 10$

c. $7a = 56$ 　　　　　　　　　**d.** $\dfrac{b}{11} = 3$

Solution

Equation	Think	Solution	Check
a. $n + 6 = 11$	What number plus 6 equals 11?	____	____ $+ 6 = 11$
b. $18 - x = 10$	_____ _____	____	$18 -$ ___ $= 10$
c. $7a = 56$	_____ _____ _____	____	$7(\_\_) = 56$
d. $\dfrac{b}{11} = 3$	_____ _____ _____	____	$\dfrac{\boxed{}}{11} = 3$

> Think of an equation as a question when solving using mental math.

✔ *Checkpoint* **Solve the equation using mental math.**

4. $x + 9 = 14$	**5.** $5t - 4 = 11$	**6.** $\dfrac{y}{4} = 15$

Homework

1.5 Use a Problem Solving Plan

Goal • Use a problem solving plan to solve problems.

VOCABULARY

Formula _____

A PROBLEM SOLVING PLAN

Use the following four-step plan to solve a problem.

Step 1 _____ Read the problem carefully. Identify what you want to know and what you want to find out.

Step 2 _____ Decide on an approach to solving the problem.

Step 3 _____ Carry out your plan. Try a new approach if the first one isn't successful.

Step 4 _____ Check that your answer is reasonable.

Example 1 *Read a problem and make a plan*

You have $7 to buy orange juice and bagels at the store. A container of juice costs $1.25 and a bagel costs $.75. If you buy two containers of juice, how many bagels can you buy?

Solution

Step 1 _____ *What do you know?* You know how much money you have and the price of a _____ and a container of juice.

What do you want to find out? You want to find out the number of _____ you can buy.

Step 2 _____ Use what you know to write a _____ that represents what you want to find out. Then write an _____ and solve it.

Example 2 Solve a problem and look back

Solve the problem in Example 1 by carrying out the plan. Then check your answer.

Solution

Step 3 _____ Write a verbal model. Then write an equation. Let b be the number of bagels you buy.

Price of juice (in dollars)	Number of containers	Price of bagel (in dollars)	Number of bagels	Cost (in dollars)
↓	↓	↓	↓	↓
____ ·	____ +	____ ·	b =	____

The equation is ____ + ____ b = ___ . One way to solve the equation is to use the strategy *guess*, *check*, and *revise*.

Guess an even number that is easily multiplied by _____. Try 4.

____ + ____ b = ___	Write equation.
____ + ____ (4) $\stackrel{?}{=}$ ___	Substitute 4 for b.
_____	Simplify; 4 _____ check.

Because _____, try an even number _____ 4. Try 6.

____ + ____ b = _	Write equation.
____ + ____ (6) $\stackrel{?}{=}$ _	Substitute 6 for b.
_____	Simplify.

For ____ you can buy ___ bagels and ___ containers of juice.

Step 4 _____ Each additional bagel you buy adds _____ to the _____ you pay for the juice. Make a table.

Bagels	0	1	2	3	4	5	6
Total Cost							

The total cost is ____ when you buy ___ bagels and ____ containers of juice. The answer in step 3 is _____ .

✓ *Checkpoint* **Complete the following exercise.**

1. Suppose in Example 1 that you have $12 and you decide to buy three containers of juice. How many bagels can you buy?

FORMULA REVIEW

Temperature

$C = \frac{5}{9}(F - 32)$, where $F =$ _____

and $C =$ _____

Simple interest

$I = Prt$, where $I =$ _____, $P =$ _____,

$r =$ _____ (as a decimal), and $t =$ _____

Distance traveled

$d = rt$, where $d =$ _____, $r =$ _____,

and $t =$ _____

Profit

$P = I - E$, where $P =$ _____, $I =$ _____, and

$E =$ _____

✓ *Checkpoint* **Complete the following exercise.**

Homework

2. In Example 1, the store where you bought the juice and bagels had an income of $7 from your purchase. The profit the store made from your purchase is $2.50. Find the store's expense for the juice and bagels.

1.6 Represent Functions as Rules and Tables

Goal • Represent functions as rules and as tables.

Your Notes

VOCABULARY

Function

Domain

Range

Independent variable

Dependent variable

Example 1 *Identify the domain and range of a function*

The input-output table shows temperatures over various increments of time. Identify the domain and range of the function.

Input (hours)	0	2	4	6
Output (°C)	24	27	30	33

Solution

Domain: _____

Range: _____

✔ *Checkpoint* **Identify the domain and range of the function.**

1.

Input	4	7	11	13
Output	10	20	35	45

Example 2   *Identify a function*

Tell whether the pairing is a function. Explain your reasoning.

Solution

Mapping diagrams are often used to represent functions. Take note of the pairings to make your decision.

a.

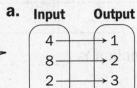

Input   Output

4 → 1
8 → 2
2 → 3

b.

Input	Output
2	2
2	4
3	6
4	8

✔ *Checkpoint* **Tell whether the pairing is a function.**

2.

Input	5	5	10	15
Output	3	4	6	8

3.

Input	0	4	12	20
Output	3	5	9	13

A function may be represented using a rule that relates one variable to another.

FUNCTIONS

| Verbal Rule | Equation | Table |

The output is 2 less than the input.

Equation: _____

Input	2	4	6	8	10
Output					

Example 3   *Make a table for a function*

The domain of the function $y = 3x$ is 0, 1, 2, and 3. Make a table for the function, then identify the range of the function.

Solution

x				
$y = 3x$				

The range of the function is _____ .

Example 4   *Write a function rule*

Write a rule for the function.

Input	3	5	7	9	11
Output	6	10	14	18	22

Solution

Let x be the input and let y be the output. Notice that each output is _____ the corresponding input. So, a rule for the function is _____ .

✅ *Checkpoint* **Write a rule for the function. Identify the domain and the range.**

Homework

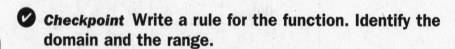

4.

Yarn (yd)	1	2	3	4
Total Cost ($)	1.5	3	4.5	6

1.7 Represent Functions as Graphs

Goal • Represent functions as graphs.

Your Notes

GRAPHING A FUNCTION

- You can use a graph to represent a _____.
- In a given table, each corresponding pair of input and output values forms an _____.
- An ordered pair of numbers can be plotted as a _____.
- The *x*-coordinate is the _____.
- The *y*-coordinate is the _____.
- The horizontal axis of the graph is labeled with the _____.
- The vertical axis is labeled with the the _____ _____.

Example 1   *Graph a function*

Graph the function *y* = *x* + 1 with domain 1, 2, 3, 4, and 5.

Solution

Step 1 Make an _____ table.

x				
y				

Step 2 Plot a point for each _____ (*x*, *y*).

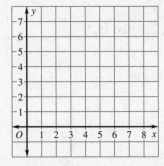

Example 2   *Write a function rule for a graph*

Write a function rule for the function represented by the graph. Identify the domain and the range of the funtion.

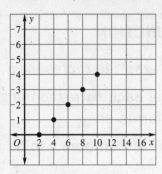

Solution

Step 1 Make a _____ for the graph.

x				
y				

Step 2 Find a _____ between the input and output values.

Step 3 Write a _____ that describes the relationship.

  $y = $ _____

A rule for the function is $y = $ _____ . The

domain of the function is _____.

The range is _____.

✔ **Checkpoint** Complete the following exercise.

1. Graph the function $y = \frac{1}{3}x + 1$ with domain 0, 3, 6, 9, and 12.

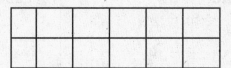

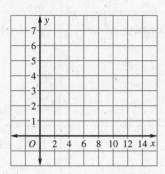

✔ **Checkpoint** Write a rule for the function represented by the graph. Identify the domain and the range of the function.

2.

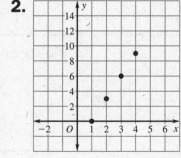

3.

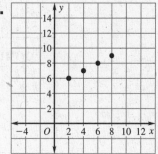

Homework

Words to Review

Give an example of the vocabulary word.

Variable	Algebraic expression
Power, Base, Exponent	Verbal model
Rate	Unit rate
Equation	Inequality
Formula	Function
Domain	Range

Review your notes and Chapter 1 by using the Chapter Review on pages 53–56 of your textbook.

2.1 Use Integers and Rational Numbers

Goal • Graph and compare positive and negative numbers.

Your Notes

VOCABULARY

Whole number

_____

Integer

_____

Rational number

_____

Opposite

_____

_____

Absolute value

_____

_____

Conditional statement

Example 1 *Graph and compare integers*

Graph −2 and −5 on a number line. Then tell which number is less.

Solution

> Negative integers are integers less than 0 and positive integers are integers greater than 0. The integer 0 is neither negative nor positive.

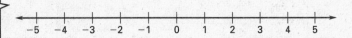

On the number line, _____ is to the left of _____.

So, _____ < _____.

Example 2 | *Classify numbers*

Tell whether each of the following numbers is a whole number, an integer, or a rational number: **3, 1.7, −14,** and $-\frac{1}{2}$.

Solution

Number	Whole Number?	Integer?	Rational Number?
3			
1.7			
−14			
$-\frac{1}{2}$			

Example 3 | *Order rational numbers*

Temperature The table shows the low daily temperatures for a town over a five-day period. Order the days from warmest to coldest.

Day	1	2	3	4	5
Temperature	0°C	10°C	−2°C	5°C	−7°C

Solution

Step 1

Graph the numbers on a number line.

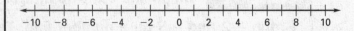

Step 2

Read the numbers from left to right:

_____.

From warmest to coldest the days are _____.

✓ Checkpoint Complete the following exercise.

---

1. Tell whether each of the following numbers is a whole number, an integer, or a rational number: 0.8, −17, −5$\frac{3}{4}$, and 2. Then order the numbers from least to greatest.

Example 4   *Find opposites of numbers*

a. If $a = -4.8$, then $-a =$ _____ = _____ .

b. If $a = \frac{5}{6}$, then $-a =$ _____ .

ABSOLUTE VALUE OF A NUMBER

Words	Numbers
If x is a positive number, then $\lvert x \rvert =$ ___ .	$\lvert 5 \rvert =$ _____
If x is 0, then $\lvert x \rvert =$ ___ .	$\lvert 0 \rvert =$ _____
If x is a _____ number, then $\lvert x \rvert = -x$.	$\lvert -4 \rvert =$ _____ = _____

Example 5   *Find absolute values of numbers*

a. If $a = -\frac{3}{7}$, then $\lvert a \rvert =$ _____ = _____ = ___ .

b. If $a = 2.9$, then $\lvert a \rvert =$ _____ = _____ .

Example 6 *Analyze a conditional statement*

Identify the hypothesis and the conclusion of the statement "If a number is an integer, then the number is positive." Tell whether the statement is *true* or *false*. If it is false, give a counterexample.

Solution

Hypothesis: _____

Conclusion: _____

The statement is _____

_____.

✓ *Checkpoint* For the given value of *a*, find $-a$ and $|a|$.

2. $a = 6$	**3.** $a = -9.5$	**4.** $a = -\dfrac{3}{8}$

✓ *Checkpoint* Identify the hypothesis and conclusion of the statement. Tell whether the statement is *true* or *false*. If it is false, give a counterexample.

5. If a number is negative, then the absolute value of the number is negative.

Homework

2.2 Add Real Numbers

Goal • Add positive and negative numbers.

Your Notes

VOCABULARY

Additive identity

Additive inverse

Example 1 *Add two integers using a number line*

Use the number line to find the sum.

a. $-5 + 7$

> Remember: To add a positive number, move to the right on a number line. To add a negative number, move to the left.

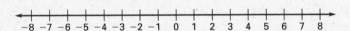

Start at _____.

To add, move _____ units to the _____.

End at ___.

Answer: $-5 + 7 =$ ___.

b. $-3 + (-4)$

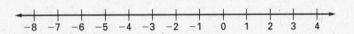

Start at _____.

To add, move _____ units to the _____.

End at _____.

Answer: $-3 + (-4) =$ _____.

RULES OF ADDITION

To add two numbers with the *same sign*:

1. Add their _____.

2. The sum has the _____ as the numbers added.

Example: $-5 + (-7) = $ _____

To add two numbers with *different signs*:

1. Subtract the _____ absolute value.

2. The sum has the _____ as the number with the _____ absolute value.

Example: $-10 + 4 = $ ____

Example 2 **Add real numbers**

Find the sum.

a. $-2.5 + (-4.2) = -($ _____ $+$ _____ $)$ Rule of same signs

$= -($ ____ $+$ ____ $)$ Take absolute values.

$= $ _____ Add.

b. $10.5 + (-15.0) = $ _____ $-$ _____ Rule of different signs

$= $ _____ $-$ _____ Take absolute values.

$= $ _____ Subtract and take sign from greater absolute value.

✓ *Checkpoint* Find the sum.

1. $-7 + (-3)$	2. $9.6 + (-2.1)$

PROPERTIES OF ADDITION

Commutative Property The order in which you add two numbers does not change the sum.

$a + b = \underline{} + \underline{}$

Example: $-1 + 3 = \underline{} + \underline{}$

Associative Property The way you group three numbers in a sum does not change the sum.

$(a + b) + c = \underline{} + (\underline{} + \underline{})$

Example: $(1 + 2) + 3 = \underline{} + (\underline{} + \underline{})$

Identity Property The sum of a number and 0 is the number.

$a + 0 = \underline{} + \underline{} = \underline{}$

Example: $4 + 0 = \underline{}$

Inverse Property The sum of a number and its opposite is 0.

$a + (-a) = \underline{} + \underline{} = \underline{}$

Example: $-9 + \underline{} = 0$

Example 3 *Identify properties of addition*

Identify the property illustrated by the statement.

Statement	Property Illustrated
a. $x + 5 = 5 + x$	_____ of addition
b. $y + 0 = y$	_____ of addition

✔ **Checkpoint** Identify the property being illustrated.

3. $-5 + 5 = 0$

4. $(-5 + 2) + 3 = -5 + (2 + 3)$

2.3 Subtract Real Numbers

Goal • Subtract real numbers.

SUBTRACTION RULE

Words: To subtract b from a, add the _____ of b to a.

Algebra: $a - b =$ ___ $+$ _____

Numbers: $15 - 7 =$ ____ $+$ _____

Example 1   *Subtract real numbers*

Find the difference.

a. $-10 - 4 = -10 +$ _____ $=$ _____

b. $13 - (-11) = 13 +$ ____ $=$ ____

Example 2   *Evaluate a variable expression*

Evaluate the expression $a - b + 5.3$ when $a = 6.5$ and $b = -3$.

Solution

$a - b + 5.3 =$ _____ $-$ _____ $+ 5.3$ Substitute values.

        $=$ ____ $+$ ___ $+ 5.3$ Add the opposite of ____.

        $=$ _____   Add.

✔ **Checkpoint** Find the difference.

1. $-4 - 8$	2. $9 - 18$

✔ *Checkpoint* Evaluate the expression when $m = 3.2$ and $t = -4$.

3. $m - t + 2$	4. $(m - 3) - t$

Example 3 *Evaluate change*

Hiking Trail A sign at the start of a hiking trail states you are 320 feet below sea level. At the end of the trail another sign states you are 880 feet above sea level. Find the change in elevation of the trail.

Solution

Step 1 **Write** a verbal model of the situation.

$$\text{Change in elevation} = \frac{\text{Elevation at}}{\underline{\hspace{1cm}} \text{ of trail}} - \frac{\text{Elevation at}}{\underline{\hspace{1cm}} \text{ of trail}}$$

Step 2 **Find** the change in elevation.

$$\text{Change in elevation} = \underline{\hspace{1cm}} - \underline{\hspace{1cm}} \qquad \text{Substitute values.}$$

$$= \underline{\hspace{1cm}} + \underline{\hspace{1cm}} \qquad \text{Add the opposite of } \underline{\hspace{1cm}}.$$

$$= \underline{\hspace{1cm}} \qquad \text{Add } \underline{\hspace{1cm}} \text{ and } \underline{\hspace{1cm}}.$$

The change in elevation is $\underline{\hspace{1cm}}$ feet.

✔ *Checkpoint* Complete the following exercise.

5. In the morning, the temperature was $-3°F$. In the afternoon, the temperature was $21°F$. What was the change in temperature?

Homework

2.4 Multiply Real Numbers

Goal • Multiply real numbers.

Your Notes

VOCABULARY

Multiplicative identity _____

THE SIGN OF A PRODUCT

The product of two real numbers with the **same sign** is _____.

Examples: $5(2) =$ _____

           $-4(-5) =$ _____

The product of two real numbers with **different signs** is _____.

Examples: $5(-3) =$ _____

           $-8(4) =$ _____

Example 1   *Multiply real numbers*

Find the product.

Solution

a. $-7(-3) =$ ____   **Same signs: product is**

                            _____.

b. $3(4)(-2) =$ ____(-2) **Multiply 3 and 4.**

          $=$ _____   **Different signs: product is**

                            _____:

c. $\frac{1}{4}(-16)(-3) =$ ____(-3) **Multiply $\frac{1}{4}$ and -16.**

          $=$ ____   **Same signs: product is**

                            _____.

✓ *Checkpoint* Find the product.

1. $-4(-6)$	2. $-3(-2)(-7)$

PROPERTIES OF MULTIPLICATION

Commutative Property The order in which two numbers are multiplied does not change the product.

$a \cdot b = \underline{} \cdot \underline{}$

Example: $3 \cdot 4 = \underline{} \cdot \underline{}$

Associative Property The way you group three numbers when multiplying does not change the product.

$(a \cdot b) \cdot c = \underline{} \cdot (\underline{} \cdot \underline{})$

Example: $(2 \cdot 3) \cdot 4 = \underline{} \cdot (\underline{} \cdot \underline{})$

Identity Property The product of a number and 1 is that number.

$a \cdot 1 = \underline{} \cdot \underline{} = \underline{}$

Example: $(-2) \cdot 1 = \underline{}$

Property of Zero The product of a number and 0 is 0.

$a \cdot 0 = \underline{} \cdot \underline{} = \underline{}$

Example: $4 \cdot \underline{} = 0$

Property of −1 The product of a number and −1 is the opposite of the number.

$a \cdot (-1) = \underline{} \cdot \underline{} = \underline{}$

Example: $-5 \cdot (-1) = \underline{}$

Example 2 *Identify properties of multiplication*

Identify the property illustrated by each expression.

Solution

Statement	Property Illustrated
a. $3 \cdot 0 = 0$	_____ _____
b. $t \cdot 1 = t$	_____ of multiplication
c. $a \cdot 3 = 3 \cdot a$	_____ of multiplication
d. $n \cdot (3 \cdot 5) = (n \cdot 3) \cdot 5$	_____ of multiplication
e. $-7(-1) = 7$	_____ _____

✓ *Checkpoint* **Identify the property illustrated.**

3. $-4 \cdot 0 = 0$

4. $6 \cdot 2 = 2 \cdot 6$

5. $(4 \cdot 5) \cdot 6 = 4 \cdot (5 \cdot 6)$

6. $4 \cdot (-1) = -4$

Example 3 *Use properties of multiplication*

Find the product $(0.5)(-2x)(6)$. Justify your steps.

Solution

$$(0.5)(-2x)(6) = (-2x)(0.5)(6) \underline{\hspace{4cm}}$$

$$= (-2x)(0.5 \cdot 6) \underline{\hspace{4cm}}$$

$$= (-2x)(3) \underline{\hspace{4cm}}$$

$$= 3 \cdot (-2x) \underline{\hspace{4cm}}$$

$$= [3 \cdot (-2)]x \underline{\hspace{4cm}}$$

$$= -6x \underline{\hspace{4cm}}$$

✓ **Checkpoint** Find the product. Justify your steps.

7. $-\dfrac{1}{2}(2)(3y)$

8. $(-2)(a)(-5)$

Homework

2.5 Apply the Distributive Property

Goal • Apply the distributive property.

Your Notes

VOCABULARY

Equivalent expressions

Distributive property

Terms

Coefficient

Constant term

Like terms

THE DISTRIBUTIVE PROPERTY

Let a, b, and c be real numbers.

Algebra

$a(b + c) = ab +$ _____

$(b + c)a = ba +$ _____

$a(b - c) = ab -$ _____

$(b - c)a = ba -$ _____

Numbers

$4(2 + 3) =$ _____ $+$ _____

$(3 + 5)2 =$ _____ $+$ _____

$7(5 - 3) =$ _____ $-$ _____

$(6 - 4)9 =$ _____ $-$ _____

Example 1   *Apply the distributive property*

Use the distributive property to write an equivalent equation.

Solution

> Be sure to distribute the factor outside of the parentheses to *all* of the numbers inside the parentheses.

a. $4(a + 3) = $ _____

b. $(a + 5)6 = $ _____

c. $3(x - 8) = $ _____

d. $(4 - x)(x) = $ _____

Example 2   *Distribute a negative number*

Use the distributive property to write an equivalent equation.

Solution

> Use the distributive property to combine like terms with variable parts. Your expression is *simplified* if there are no grouping symbols and all like terms are combined.

a. $-3(7 + x)$

$= $ _____$(7) + $ _____(x) **Distribute** _____.

$= $ _____   _____.

b. $(6 - a)(-2a)$

$= 6($_____$) - a($_____$)$ **Distribute** _____.

$= $ _____   _____.

✓ **Checkpoint**   Use the distributive property to write an equivalent equation.

1. $5(n + 4)$	**2.** $-a(3 + a)$

| Example 3 | *Identify parts of an expression* |

Identify the terms, like terms, coefficients, and constant terms of the expression $2x - 5 + 8x - 3$.

Solution

_____   Write the expression as a sum.

Terms: Like terms:

_____   _____

Coefficients: Constant terms:

_____   _____

✔ *Checkpoint* Identify the terms, like terms, coefficients, and constant terms of the expressions.

3. $10 + 3a - 4 - 6a$

_____

4. $7y - 11 - 4y - 1$

Homework

2.6 Divide Real Numbers

Goal • Divide real numbers.

Your Notes

VOCABULARY

Multiplicative inverse

INVERSE PROPERTY OF MULTIPLICATION

Words

The _____ of a nonzero number and its multiplicative inverse is ___ .

Algebra

$a \cdot \dfrac{1}{a} =$ ___ , $a \neq$ ___

Numbers

$4 \cdot \dfrac{1}{4} =$ ___

Example 1 *Find multiplicative inverses of numbers*

Identify the multiplicative inverse and justify your answer.

Solution

Number	Multiplicative inverse	Reason
a. 9	_____	_____
b. $-\dfrac{5}{6}$	_____	_____

✔ Checkpoint Find the multiplicative inverse.

1. $-\dfrac{2}{3}$	2. 3

DIVISION RULE

Words

To divide a number a by a nonzero number b, multiply ___ by the multiplicative inverse of ___.

Algebra

$a \div b = a \cdot \underline{\quad}$, $b \neq$ ___

Numbers

$7 \div 3 = \underline{\quad}$

> You cannot divide a real number by 0, because 0 does not have a multiplicative inverse.

THE SIGN OF A QUOTIENT

The quotient of two real numbers with the same sign is _____.

The quotient of two real numbers with different signs is _____.

The quotient of 0 and any nonzero real number is ___.

Example 2 *Divide real numbers*

Find the quotient.

Solution

a. $25 \div 5 = 25 \cdot \underline{\quad} = \underline{\quad}$

b. $-40 \div \dfrac{2}{3} = -40 \cdot \underline{\quad} = \underline{\quad}$

✓ *Checkpoint* **Find the quotient.**

3. $\dfrac{1}{2} \div \dfrac{3}{4}$	4. $16 \div \left(-\dfrac{1}{4}\right)$

Example 3 *Simplify an expression*

Simplify the expression $\dfrac{48y - 32}{8}$.

Solution

$$\dfrac{48y - 32}{8} = (48y - 32) \div \underline{\quad}$$ Rewrite fraction as division.

$$= (48y - 32) \cdot \underline{\quad}$$ Division rule

$$= 48y \cdot \underline{\quad} - 32 \cdot \underline{\quad}$$ Distributive property

$$= \underline{\qquad}$$ Simplify.

✓ *Checkpoint* **Simplify the expression.**

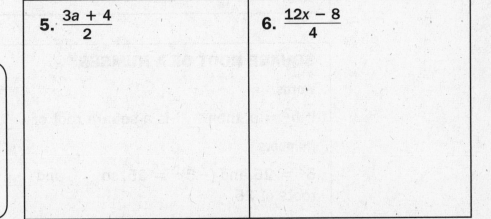

5. $\dfrac{3a + 4}{2}$	6. $\dfrac{12x - 8}{4}$

Homework

2.7 Find Square Roots and Compare Real Numbers

Goal • Find square roots and compare real numbers.

Your Notes

<table>
<tr><td colspan="2">VOCABULARY</td></tr>
<tr><td>Square root</td><td></td></tr>
<tr><td>Radicand</td><td></td></tr>
<tr><td>Perfect square</td><td></td></tr>
<tr><td>Irrational number</td><td></td></tr>
<tr><td>Real number</td><td></td></tr>
</table>

SQUARE ROOT OF A NUMBER

Words

If $b^2 = a$, then ____ is a square root of ____.

Numbers

$5^2 = 25$ and $(-5)^2 = 25$, so ____ and _____ are square roots of 25.

Example 1 *Find square roots*

Evaluate the expression.

Solution

a. $-\sqrt{36} =$ _____   The negative square root of 36 is _____.

b. $\sqrt{16} =$ ___   The positive square root of 16 is ___.

c. $\pm\sqrt{64} =$ _____   The positive and negative square roots of 64 are ___ and _____.

✓ **Checkpoint** **Evaluate the expression.**

1. $\sqrt{100}$	2. $-\sqrt{1}$

Example 2 *Classify numbers*

Tell whether each of the following numbers is a real number, a rational number, an irrational number, an integer, or a whole number: $\sqrt{144}$, $-\sqrt{49}$, $\sqrt{32}$.

Solution

Number	Real Number?	Rational Number?	Irrational Number?	Integer?	Whole Number?
$\sqrt{144}$					
$-\sqrt{49}$					
$\sqrt{32}$					

Example 3 *Graph and order real numbers*

Order the numbers from least to greatest:

$$\sqrt{16},\ \frac{5}{2},\ \sqrt{4},\ -3,\ -\sqrt{6}.$$

Solution

Graph the numbers on a number line.

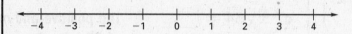

Read the numbers from left to right:

_____.

✔ *Checkpoint* **Complete the following exercises.**

3. Tell whether each of the following numbers is a real number, rational number, irrational number, integer, or whole number: $\sqrt{49},\ 0,\ -\frac{6}{4},\ -2,\ \sqrt{17}$.

---

4. Order the numbers from Exercise 3 from least to greatest.

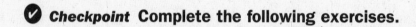

Words to Review

Give an example of the vocabulary word.

Whole number	Integer
Rational number	Opposite
Absolute Value	Conditional Statement
Additive identity/ Additive inverse	Multiplicative identity
Equivalent expressions	Distributive property
Terms	Coefficient
Constant term	Like terms

Multiplicative inverse	Square root
Radicand	Perfect square
Irrational number	Real number

Review your notes and Chapter 2 by using the Chapter Review on pages 121–124 of your textbook.

3.1 Solve One-Step Equations

Goal • Solve one-step equations using algebra.

Your Notes

VOCABULARY

Inverse operations

Equivalent equations

ADDITION PROPERTY OF EQUALITY

Words   Adding the same number to each side of an equation produces an _____.

Algebra   If $x - a = b$, then $x - a + a = $ ___ $+$ ___ or $x = $ ___ $+$ ___.

SUBTRACTION PROPERTY OF EQUALITY

Words   Subtracting the same number from each side of an equation produces an _____ _____.

Algebra   If $x + a = b$, then $x + a - a = $ ___ $-$ ___ or $x = $ ___ $-$ ___.

	Example 1 *Solve an equation using subtraction*

Solve $y + 3 = 10$.

Solution

$y + 3 = 10$	Write original equation.
$y + 3 - \underline{} = 10 - \underline{}$	Use subtraction property of equality: Subtract ____ from each side.
$y = \underline{}$	Simplify.

The solution is ____.

CHECK

$y + 3 = 10$	Write original equation.
$\underline{} + 3 \stackrel{?}{=} 10$	Substitute ____ for y.
$\underline{} = 10 \checkmark$	Solution checks.

> Remember to check your solution in the original equation for accuracy.

	Example 2 *Solve an equation using addition*

Solve $t - 9 = 11$.

Solution

$t - 9 = 11$	Write original equation.
$t - 9 + \underline{} = 11 + \underline{}$	Use addition property of equality: Add ____ to each side.
$t = \underline{}$	Simplify.

The solution is ____.

CHECK

$t - 9 = 11$	Write original equation.
$\underline{} - 9 \stackrel{?}{=} 11$	Substitute ____ for t.
$\underline{} = 11 \checkmark$	Solution checks.

✔ **Checkpoint** Solve each equation. Check your solution.

1. $a + 6 = 17$	**2.** $b - 17 = 12$
3. $-3 = x + 2$	**4.** $y - 4 = -6$

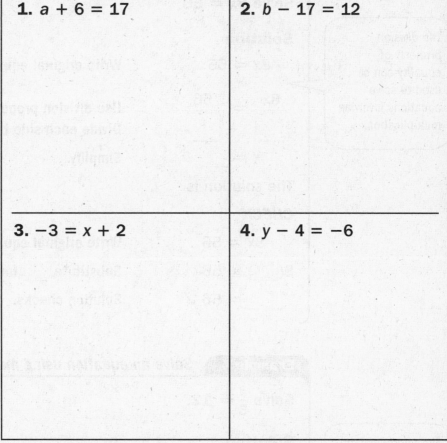

MULTIPLICATION PROPERTY OF EQUALITY

Words   Multiplying each side of an equation by the same non-zero number produces an

_____.

Algebra   If $\frac{x}{a} = b$ and $a \neq 0$, then $a \cdot \frac{x}{a} = $ ____ $\cdot$ ____

or $x = $ _____.

DIVISION PROPERTY OF EQUALITY

Words   Dividing each side of an equation by the same non-zero number produces an _____

_____.

Algebra   If $ax = b$, and $a \neq 0$, then $\frac{ax}{a} = \dfrac{\boxed{}}{\boxed{}}$ or $x = \dfrac{\boxed{}}{\boxed{}}$.

Example 3   *Solve an equation using division*

Solve $8x = 56$.

Solution

> The *division property of equality* can be used to solve equations involving multiplication.

$8x = 56$	Write original equation.
$\dfrac{8x}{\boxed{}} = \dfrac{56}{\boxed{}}$	Use division property of equality: Divide each side by ___.
$x = \underline{}$	Simplify.

The solution is ___.

CHECK

$8x = 56$	Write original equation.
$8(\underline{}) \overset{?}{=} 56$	Substitute ___ for *x*.
$\underline{} = 56 \checkmark$	Solution checks.

Example 4   *Solve an equation using multiplication*

Solve $\dfrac{a}{5} = 12$.

Solution

> The *multiplication property of equality* can be used to solve equations involving division.

$\dfrac{a}{5} = 12$	Write original equation.
$\underline{} \cdot \dfrac{a}{5} = \underline{} \cdot 12$	Use multiplication property of equality: Multiply each side by ___.
$a = \underline{}$	Simplify.

The solution is ___.

CHECK

$\dfrac{a}{5} = 12$	Write original equation.
$\dfrac{\boxed{}}{5} \overset{?}{=} 12$	Substitute ___ for *a*.
$\underline{} = 12 \checkmark$	Solution checks.

Example 5 *Solve an equation by multiplying by a reciprocal*

Solve $\frac{3}{5}t = 6$.

Solution

The coefficient of t is $\frac{3}{5}$. The reciprocal of $\frac{3}{5}$ is ____ .

$\frac{3}{5}t = 6$ Write original equation.

$\underline{\quad} \cdot \frac{3}{5}t = \underline{\quad} \cdot 6$ Multiply each side by the reciprocal ____ .

$t = \underline{\quad}$ Simplify.

The solution is ____ .

CHECK

$\frac{3}{5}t = 6$ Write original equation.

$\frac{3}{5}(\underline{\quad}) \stackrel{?}{=} 6$ Substitute ____ for t.

$\underline{\quad} = 6 \checkmark$ Solution checks.

✔ **Checkpoint** Solve each equation. Check your solution.

5. $3x = 39$	**6.** $\frac{b}{4} = 13$
7. $-24 = 4x$	**8.** $-\frac{3}{8}m = 21$

Homework

3.2 Solve Two-Step Equations

Goal • Solve two-step equations.

Your Notes

IDENTIFYING OPERATIONS

Identify the operations involved in the equation
$3x + 7 = 19$.

Operations performed on x	Operations to isolate x
1. Multiply by ____.	1. Subtract ____.
2. Add ____.	2. Divide by ____.

Example 1 **Solve a two-step equation**

Solve $3x + 7 = 19$.

Solution

> When solving a two-step equation, apply the inverse operations in the reverse order of the order of operations.

$$3x + 7 = 19$$ **Write original equation.**

$$3x + 7 - \underline{\quad} = 19 - \underline{\quad}$$ **Subtract ____ from each side.**

$$3x = \underline{\quad}$$ **Simplify.**

$$\frac{3x}{\boxed{\quad}} = \frac{12}{\boxed{\quad}}$$ **Divide each side by ____.**

$$x = \underline{\quad}$$ **Simplify.**

The solution is ____.

CHECK

$$3x + 7 = 19$$ **Write original equation.**

$$3(\underline{\quad}) + 7 \stackrel{?}{=} 19$$ **Substitute ____ for x.**

$$\underline{\quad} + 7 \stackrel{?}{=} 19$$ **Multiply 3 by ____.**

$$\underline{\quad} = 19 \checkmark$$ **Simplify. Solution checks.**

✔ **Checkpoint** Solve the two-step equation. Check your solution.

1. $\frac{r}{4} - 12 = -5$	2. $7k - 14 = 42$

Example 2 *Solve a two-step equation by combining like terms*

Solve $4a + 3a = 63$.

Solution

$4a + 3a = 63$	Write original equation.
$\underline{\hspace{1cm}} = 63$	Combine like terms.
$\dfrac{\boxed{}}{\boxed{}} = \dfrac{63}{\boxed{}}$	Divide each side by ___.
$a = \underline{\hspace{0.5cm}}$	Simplify.

The solution is ___.

CHECK

$4a + 3a = 63$	Write original equation.
$4(\underline{\hspace{0.5cm}}) + 3(\underline{\hspace{0.5cm}}) \stackrel{?}{=} 63$	Substitute ___ for a.
$\underline{\hspace{1cm}} + \underline{\hspace{1cm}} \stackrel{?}{=} 63$	Multiply 4 by ___ and 3 by ___.
$\underline{\hspace{1cm}} = 63$ ✓	Add. Solution checks.

✔ **Checkpoint** Solve the equation. Check your solution.

3. $5z + 4z = 36$	4. $5b - 2b = 9$

Example 3   *Find an input of a function*

The output of a function is 2 more than 4 times the input. Find the input when the output is 14.

Solution

Step 1 **Write** an equation for the function. Let *x* be the input and *y* be the output.

       y = _____   *y* is 2 more than 4 times *x*.

Step 2 **Solve** the equation when *y* = 14.

       y = _____   **Write original function.**

   _____ = _____   **Substitute** ____ **for** *y*.

   _____ = _____   **Subtract** ____ **from each side.**

       ____ = ____   **Simplify.**

   $\dfrac{\boxed{}}{\boxed{}} = \dfrac{\boxed{}}{\boxed{}}$ **Divide each side by** ___.

       ____ = *x*   **Simplify.**

An input of ___ produces an output of _____.

CHECK

       y = _____   **Write original function.**

   ____ $\overset{?}{=}$ _____   **Substitute** _____ **for** *y* **and** ___ **for** *x*.

   ____ $\overset{?}{=}$ _____   **Multiply** ____ **and** ___.

   ____ = _____ ✓   **Simplify. Solution checks.**

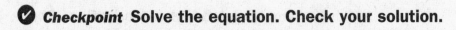

✔ *Checkpoint* Solve the equation. Check your solution.

5. The output of a function is 3 less than 6 times the input. Find the input when the output is 15.

3.3 Solve Multi-Step Equations

Goal • Solve multi-step equations.

Your Notes

Example 1 **Solve an equation by combining like terms**

Solve $3t + 5t - 5 = 11$.

Solution

$$3t + 5t - 5 = 11 \qquad \text{Write original equation.}$$

$$\underline{\quad\quad} - 5 = 11 \qquad \text{Combine like terms.}$$

$$\underline{\quad\quad} - 5 + \underline{\quad} = 11 + \underline{\quad} \qquad \text{Add } \underline{\quad} \text{ to each side.}$$

$$\underline{\quad} = \underline{\quad} \qquad \text{Simplify.}$$

$$\frac{\boxed{}}{\boxed{}} = \frac{\boxed{}}{\boxed{}} \qquad \text{Divide each side by } \underline{\quad}.$$

$$t = \underline{\quad} \qquad \text{Simplify.}$$

The solution is $\underline{\quad}$.

Example 2 **Solve an equation using the distributive property**

Solve $5a + 3(a + 2) = 22$.

Solution

Method 1	Method 2
Show All Steps	Do Some Steps Mentally

Method 1:

$$5a + 3(a + 2) = 22$$
$$5a + \underline{\quad} + \underline{\quad} = 22$$
$$\underline{\quad} + \underline{\quad} = 22$$
$$\underline{\quad\quad\quad} = 22 - \underline{\quad}$$
$$\underline{\quad} = 16$$
$$\frac{\boxed{}}{\boxed{}} = \frac{16}{\boxed{}}$$
$$a = \underline{\quad}$$

Method 2:

$$5a + 3(a + 2) = 22$$
$$5a + \underline{\quad} + \underline{\quad} = 22$$
$$\underline{\quad} + \underline{\quad} = 22$$
$$\underline{\quad} = 16$$
$$a = \underline{\quad}$$

Copyright © McDougal Littell/Houghton Mifflin Company.

Lesson 3.3 • Algebra 1 Notetaking Guide **55**

✔ *Checkpoint* **Solve the equation. Check your solution.**

1. $9d - 4d - 2 = 18$	**2.** $2x + 7(x - 3) = 6$
3. $3w + 4 + w = 36$	**4.** $40 = 2(10 + 4k) + 2k$

Example 3   *Multiply by a reciprocal to solve an equation*

Solve $\frac{3}{4}(a - 5) = 9$.

Solution

$$\frac{3}{4}(a - 5) = 9 \qquad \text{Write original equation.}$$

$$\underline{\quad} \cdot \frac{3}{4}(a - 5) = \underline{\quad} \cdot 9 \quad \text{Multiply each side by } \underline{\quad}.$$

$$a - 5 = \underline{\quad} \qquad \text{Simplify.}$$

$$a - 5 + \underline{\quad} = 12 + \underline{\quad} \quad \text{Add } \underline{\quad} \text{ to each side.}$$

$$a = \underline{\quad} \qquad \text{Simplify.}$$

✔ *Checkpoint* **Solve the equation. Check your solution.**

5. $\frac{1}{2}(4x - 2) = 7$	**6.** $\frac{5}{6}(2y + 4) = 10$

Homework

3.4 Solve Equations with Variables on Both Sides

Goal • Solve equations with variables on both sides.

Your Notes

> **VOCABULARY**
>
> Identity

Example 1   Solve an equation with variables on both sides

Solve $15 + 4a = 9a - 5$.

Solution

> Collect variables on one side of the equation and constant terms on the other to solve equations with variables on both sides.

$$15 + 4a = 9a - 5$$ Write original equation.

$$15 + 4a - \underline{\quad} = 9a - \underline{\quad} - 5$$ Subtract _____ from each side.

$$15 = \underline{\quad} - 5$$ Simplify.

$$15 + \underline{\quad} = \underline{\quad} - 5 + \underline{\quad}$$ Add _____ to each side.

$$\underline{\quad} = \underline{\quad}$$ Simplify.

$$\frac{\boxed{}}{\boxed{}} = \frac{\boxed{}}{\boxed{}}$$ Divide each side by _____.

$$\underline{\quad} = a$$ Simplify.

The solution is _____.

CHECK

$$15 + 4a = 9a - 5$$ Write original equation.

$$15 + 4(\underline{\quad}) \stackrel{?}{=} 9(\underline{\quad}) - 5$$ Substitute _____ for a.

$$15 + \underline{\quad} \stackrel{?}{=} \underline{\quad} - 5$$ Multiply.

$$\underline{\quad} = \underline{\quad} \checkmark$$ Solution checks.

Example 2 *Solve an equation with grouping symbols*

Solve $4t - 12 = 6(t + 3)$.

Solution

$4t - 12 = 6(t + 3)$	Write original equation.
$4t - 12 = \underline{\quad} + \underline{\quad}$	Distributive property
$-12 = \underline{\quad} + \underline{\quad}$	Subtract _____ from each side.
$\underline{\quad} = \underline{\quad}$	Subtract _____ from each side.
$\underline{\quad} = t$	Divide each side by ___.

✔ **Checkpoint** Solve the equation. Check your solution.

1. $3b + 7 = 8b + 2$	**2.** $6d - 6 = \frac{3}{4}(4d + 8)$

Example 3 *Identify the number of solutions of an equation*

Solve the equation, if possible.

a. $4x + 5 = 4(x + 5)$ b. $6x - 3 = 3(2x - 1)$

Solution

a. $4x + 5 = 4(x + 5)$ Original equation

   $4x + 5 = \underline{\qquad}$ Distributive property

The equation $4x + 5 = \underline{\qquad}$ is _____ because the number $4x$ _____ equal to 5 more than itself and _____ more than itself. So, the equation has _____ solution.

b. $6x - 3 = 3(2x - 1)$ Original equation

   $6x - 3 = \underline{\qquad}$ Distributive property

The statement $6x - 3 = \underline{\qquad}$ is _____ for all values of x. So, the equation is an _____.

✔ *Checkpoint* Solve the equation, if possible.

3. $\frac{1}{2}(4t - 6) = 2t$

---

4. $10m - 4 = -2(2 - 5m)$

STEPS FOR SOLVING LINEAR EQUATIONS

Step 1 Use the _____ to remove any grouping symbols.

Step 2 _____ the expression on each side of the equation.

Step 3 Use the properties of equality to collect the _____ terms on one side of the equation and the _____ terms on the other side of the equation.

Step 4 Use the properties of equality to solve for the _____.

Step 5 Check your _____ in the original equation.

Homework

3.5 Write Ratios and Proportions

Goals • Find ratios and write and solve proportions.

VOCABULARY

Ratio _____

_____

Proportion

RATIOS

1. A ratio uses _____ to compare two quantities.

2. The ratio of two quantities, *a* and *b*, where *b* is not equal to 0, can be written in three ways:

   _____   _____   _____

3. Each ratio is read "the _____ of *a* to *b*".

4. Ratios should be written in _____ form.

Example 1 *Write a ratio*

Cell Phone Use A person makes 6 long distance calls and 15 local calls in 1 month.

a. Find the ratio of long distance calls to local calls.

b. Find the ratio of long distance calls to all calls.

Solution

a. $\dfrac{\text{long distance calls}}{\text{local calls}} = \dfrac{\boxed{}}{\boxed{}} = \dfrac{\boxed{}}{\boxed{}}$

b. $\dfrac{\text{long distance calls}}{\text{all calls}} = \dfrac{\boxed{}}{\boxed{}} = \dfrac{\boxed{}}{\boxed{}}$

✅ *Checkpoint* **Shawn and Myra are selling tickets to their school's talent show. Shawn sold 36 tickets, and Myra sold 44 tickets. Find the specified ratio.**

---

1. The number of tickets Shawn sold to the number of tickets Myra sold

---

2. The number of tickets Myra sold to the number of tickets Shawn and Myra sold

---

Example 2 *Solve a proportion*

Solve the proportion $\frac{y}{15} = \frac{3}{5}$.

> Use the same methods for solving equations to solve proportions with a variable in the numerator.

Solution

$\frac{y}{15} = \frac{3}{5}$ **Write original proportion.**

___ $\cdot \frac{y}{15} =$ ___ $\cdot \frac{3}{5}$ **Multiply each side by ___ .**

$y = \dfrac{\boxed{}}{\boxed{}}$ **Simplify.**

$y =$ ___   **Divide.**

✅ *Checkpoint* **Solve the proportion. Check your solution.**

3. $\frac{9}{4} = \frac{c}{28}$	**4.** $\frac{a}{32} = \frac{7}{8}$

Example 3 *Solve a multi-step problem*

Swimming Pool A empty swimming pool is being filled with water. After 5 minutes the pool has 400 gallons of water. If the pool has a volume of 11,200 gallons, how long does it take to fill the empty pool?

Solution

Step 1 Write a proportion involving two ratios that compare the amount of water in the pool to the amount of time.

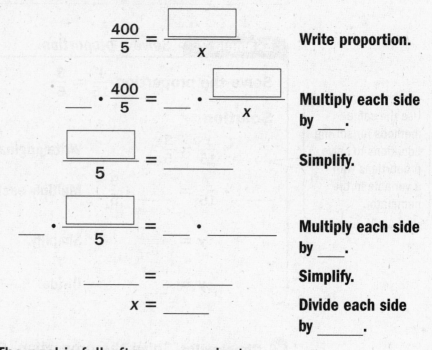

$$\frac{400}{5} = \frac{\boxed{}}{x} \quad \begin{array}{l}\leftarrow \text{ gallons} \\ \leftarrow \text{ minutes}\end{array}$$

Step 2 Solve the proportion.

$$\frac{400}{5} = \frac{\boxed{}}{x}$$ Write proportion.

$$\underline{} \cdot \frac{400}{5} = \underline{} \cdot \frac{\boxed{}}{x}$$ Multiply each side by ___.

$$\frac{\boxed{}}{5} = \underline{}$$ Simplify.

$$\underline{} \cdot \frac{\boxed{}}{5} = \underline{} \cdot \underline{}$$ Multiply each side by ___.

$$\underline{} = \underline{}$$ Simplify.

$$x = \underline{}$$ Divide each side by _____.

The pool is full after _____ minutes.

✔ *Checkpoint* **Complete the following exercise.**

5. An Olympic sized pool has a volume of 810,000 gallons. If it is filled at the same rate as the pool in Example 3, how long will it take to fill the pool?

3.6 Solve Proportions Using Cross Products

 Goal • Solve proportions using cross products.

Your Notes

VOCABULARY

Cross product

Scale drawing

Scale model

Scale

CROSS PRODUCTS PROPERTY

Words The cross products of a proportion
are _____ .

Example $\dfrac{5}{6} = \dfrac{10}{12}$ _____ • 10 = 60
_____ • 12 = 60

Algebra If $\dfrac{a}{b} = \dfrac{c}{d}$ where $b \neq 0$ and $d \neq 0$, then
$ad =$ ____ .

Your Notes

| Example 1 | Solve a proportion using cross products |

Solve the proportion $\frac{5}{y} = \frac{15}{75}$.

Solution

$\frac{5}{y} = \frac{15}{75}$ Write original proportion.

$\underline{\quad} \cdot 75 = \underline{\quad} \cdot 15$ Cross products property

$\underline{\quad\quad} = \underline{\quad\quad}$ Simplify.

$\underline{\quad\quad} = y$ Divide each side by $\underline{\quad}$.

The solution is $\underline{\quad}$.

| Example 2 | Write and solve a proportion |

Plant Food To feed your plants, you need to mix 3 tablespoons of plant food with 16 ounces of water. If it takes 80 ounces of water to feed all of your plants, how many tablespoons of plant food are needed?

Solution

Step 1 Write a proportion involving two ratios that compare the amount of plant food with the amount of water.

$\frac{3}{16} = \frac{x}{\boxed{\quad}}$ ← amount of plant food
← amount of water

Step 2 Solve the proportion.

$\frac{3}{16} = \frac{x}{\boxed{\quad}}$ Write proportion.

$3 \cdot \underline{\quad} = \underline{\quad} \cdot x$ Cross product property

$\underline{\quad\quad} = \underline{\quad\quad}$ Simplify.

$\underline{\quad\quad} = x$ Divide each side by $\underline{\quad}$.

You need $\underline{\quad}$ tablespoons of plant food for 80 ounces of water.

✓ *Checkpoint* **Solve the proportion. Check your solution.**

---

1. $\dfrac{5}{n} = \dfrac{25}{45}$ **2.** $\dfrac{6}{b} = \dfrac{3}{b-2}$

---

3. In Example 2, suppose it takes 120 ounces to feed all of the plants. How many tablespoons of plant food are needed?

Example 3   *Use a scale model*

Scale Model An architect creates a scale model of a school. The school is 50 feet high. The ratio of the model to the actual school is 1 foot to 75 feet. Estimate the height of the model.

Solution

Write and solve a proportion to find the height h of the scale model.

$$\dfrac{1}{\boxed{}} = \dfrac{h}{\boxed{}} \quad \leftarrow \text{ height of model (feet)}$$
$$\qquad\qquad\qquad \leftarrow \text{ actual height (feet)}$$

$1 \cdot \underline{} = \underline{} \cdot h$ **Cross products property**

$\underline{} = h$ **Simplify.**

The height of the scale model is $\underline{}$ foot, or $\underline{}$ inches.

✓ *Checkpoint* **Complete the following exercise.**

Homework

4. In Example 3, suppose the ratio of the model to the actual school is 1 foot to 100 feet. Estimate the height of the model.

3.7 Solve Percent Problems

Goal • Solve percent problems.

SOLVING PERCENT PROBLEMS USING PROPORTIONS

You can represent "*a* is *p* percent of *b*" by using the proportion

$$\frac{a}{b} = \frac{p}{\boxed{}}$$

where *a* is a part of the base ____ and $\dfrac{p}{\boxed{}}$, or *p*%, is the _____.

Example 1   *Find a percent using a proportion*

What percent of 50 is 33?

Solution

Write a proportion when 50 is the base and 33 is part of the base.

$\dfrac{a}{b} = \dfrac{p}{100}$ **Write proportion.**

$\dfrac{\boxed{}}{\boxed{}} = \dfrac{p}{100}$ **Substitute ____ for *a* and ____ for *b*.**

_____ = 50*p*   **Cross products property**

_____ = *p*   **Divide each side by ____.**

33 is _____ of 50.

✔ **Checkpoint** **Use a proportion to answer the question.**

1. What percent of 80 is 28?

---

2. What percent of 90 is 36?

THE PERCENT EQUATION

You can represent "a is p percent of b" by using the equation:

$$a = \underline{\quad} \cdot b$$

where a is a part of the base ___ and $p\%$ is the _____ .

Example 2 **Find a percent using the percent equation**

What percent of 224 is 98?

The percent equation, $a = p\% \cdot b$, is derived from the proportion, $\dfrac{a}{b} = \dfrac{p}{100}$.

Solution

$a = p\% \cdot b$	Write percent equation.
$\underline{\quad} = p\% \cdot \underline{\quad}$	Substitute ___ for a and ___ for b.
$\underline{\quad\quad} = p\%$	Divide each side by ___ .
$\underline{\quad\quad} = p\%$	Write decimal as a percent.

98 is _____ of 224.

CHECK

$\underline{\quad} = p\% \cdot \underline{\quad}$	Write original equation.
$\underline{\quad} \overset{?}{=} \underline{\quad\quad} \cdot \underline{\quad}$	Substitute _____ for $p\%$.
$\underline{\quad} = \underline{\quad}$ ✓	Multiply. Solution checks.

Example 3   *Find a part of a base using the percent equation*

What number is 75% of 164?

Solution

$a = p\% \cdot b$	Write percent equation.
$= \underline{\hspace{1cm}} \cdot \underline{\hspace{1cm}}$	Substitute \underline{\hspace{1cm}} for p and \underline{\hspace{1cm}} for b.
$= \underline{\hspace{1cm}} \cdot \underline{\hspace{1cm}}$	Write percent as a decimal.
$= \underline{\hspace{1cm}}$	Multiply.

\underline{\hspace{1.5cm}} is 75% of 164.

✔ *Checkpoint* **Use the percent equation to answer the question.**

3. What percent of 76 is 57?

_____

4. What number is 35% of 80?

Example 4   *Find a base using the percent equation*

21 is 37.5% of what number?

Solution

$a = p\% \cdot b$	Write percent equation.
$\underline{\hspace{1cm}} = \underline{\hspace{1cm}} \cdot b$	Substitute \underline{\hspace{1cm}} for a and \underline{\hspace{1cm}} for p.
$\underline{\hspace{1cm}} = \underline{\hspace{1cm}} \cdot b$	Write percent as a decimal.
$\underline{\hspace{1cm}} = b$	Divide each side by \underline{\hspace{1cm}}.

21 is 75% of \underline{\hspace{1cm}}.

✓ *Checkpoint* **Use the percent equation to answer the question.**

5. 27 is 25% of what number?

---

6. 78 is 150% of what number?

TYPES OF PERCENT PROBLEMS

Percent Problem	Example	Equation
Find a percent.	What percent of 252 is 84?	_____ = p% · _____
Find part of a base.	What number is 30% of 90?	a = _____ · _____
Find a base.	16 is 20% of what number?	16 = _____ · b

3.8 Rewrite Equations and Formulas

Goal • Write equations in function form and rewrite formulas.

Your Notes

VOCABULARY

Function form

Literal equation

Example 1   *Rewrite an equation in function form*

Write 2x + 2y = 10 in function form.

Solution

Solve the equation for y.

2x + 2y = 10	Write original equation.
2y = _____	Subtract _____ from each side.
y = _____	Divide each side by ___.

The equation y = _____ is written in function form.

Example 2   *Solve a literal equation*

Solve a + by = c for a.

Solution

a + by = c	Write original equation.
a = _____	Subtract _____ from each side.

The solution is a = _____.

Example 3 *Solve and use a formula*

The interest *I* on an investment of *P* dollars at an interest rate *r* for *t* years is given by the formula $I = Prt$.

a. Solve the formula for the time *t*.

b. Use the rewritten formula to find the time it takes to earn $100 interest on $1000 at a rate of 5.0%.

Solution

a. $I = Prt$ Write original formula.

$\dfrac{I}{\boxed{}} = t$ Divide each side by ____.

b. Substitute _____ for *I*, _____ for *P*, and _____ for *r* in the rewritten formula.

$t = \dfrac{I}{\boxed{}}$ Write rewritten formula.

$= \dfrac{\boxed{}}{\boxed{} \cdot \boxed{}}$ Substitute.

$= \underline{}$ Simplify.

It will take ___ years to earn $100 in interest.

✔ *Checkpoint* Write the equation in function form.

1. $2x + y = 5$	**2.** $3 + 3y = 9 - 6x$

✔ *Checkpoint* Complete the following exercises.

3. Solve $a + by = c$ for *b*.

4. In Example 3, solve the equation for *P*. Find the investment *P* if $I = \$400$, $r = 4\%$, and $t = 4$ years.

Words to Review

Give an example of the vocabulary word.

Inverse operations	Equivalent equations
Identity	Ratio
Proportion	Cross product
Scale drawing	Scale model
Scale	Function form
Literal equation	

Review your notes and Chapter 3 by using the Chapter Review on pages 192–196 of your textbook.

4.1 Plot Points in a Coordinate Plane

Goal • Identify and plot points in a coordinate plane.

Your Notes

VOCABULARY

Quadrant

Example 1 *Name points in a coordinate plane*

Give the coordinates of the point.

a. *A*   b. *B*

Solution

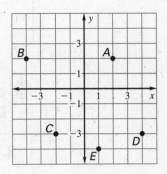

a. Point *A* is ____ units to the
   _____ of the origin and
   ____ units _____.
   The *x*-coordinate is ____.
   The *y*-coordinate is ____.
   The coordinates are _____.

> Points in Quadrant I have two positive coordinates. Points in the other three quadrants have at least one negative coordinate.

b. Point *B* is ____ units to the
   _____ of the origin and
   ____ units _____.
   The *x*-coordinate is _____.
   The *y*-coordinate is ____.
   The coordinates are _____.

✔ *Checkpoint* **Complete the following exercise.**

1. Use the coordinate plane in Example 1 to give the coordinates of points *C*, *D*, and *E*.

Example 2   *Plot points in a coordinate plane*

Plot the point in a coordinate plane. Describe the location of the point.

a. *A*(0, 3)　　　　　b. *B*(1, −2)　　　　　c. *C*(−3, −4)

Solution

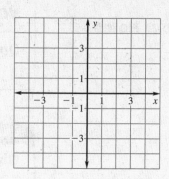

a. Begin at the _____.
   Move ___ units _____.
   Point *A* is on the _____.

b. Begin at the _____.
   Move ___ unit to the _____.
   Move ___ units _____.
   Point *B* is in Quadrant ____.

c. Begin at the _____
   Move ___ units to the _____.
   Move ___ units _____.
   Point *C* is in Quadrant ____.

✔ *Checkpoint* **Plot the point in a coordinate plane. Describe the location of the point.**

2. *A*(−4, −4)	3. *B*(2, 0)
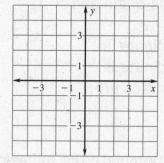	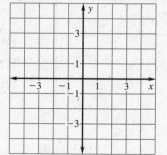

Example 3 *Graph a function*

Graph the function $y = x + 1$ with domain -2, -1, 0, 1, 2. Then identify the range of the function.

Solution

Step 1 Make a table.

x	$y = x + 1$
-2	$y = -2 + 1 =$ _____
-1	$y = -1 + 1 =$ _____
0	$y = 0 + 1 =$ _____
1	$y = 1 + 1 =$ _____
2	$y = 2 + 1 =$ _____

Step 2 List the ordered pairs:

$(-2,$ _____ $), (-1,$ _____ $), (0,$ _____ $), (1,$ _____ $), (2,$ _____ $).$

Then graph the function.

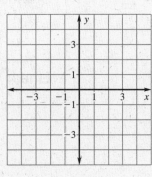

Step 3 Identify the range: _____.

✔ *Checkpoint* Complete the following exercise.

4. Graph the function $y = -\dfrac{1}{2}x + 3$ with domain

   -4, -2, 0, 2, and 4. Then identify the range.

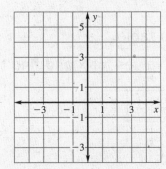

Homework

4.2 Graph Linear Equations

Goal • Graph linear equations in a coordinate plane.

VOCABULARY

Solution of an equation in two variables

_____

Graph of an equation in two variables

_____

Linear equation

Standard form of a linear equation

_____

Linear function

Example 1   *Graph an equation*

Graph the equation $x + y = 4$.

Solution

Step 1 Solve the equation for y.

$x + y = 4$

$y =$ _____

Step 2 Make a table.

Choose a few values for x and find the values for y.

x	-2	-1	0	1	2
y					

> Use convenient values for x when making a table. These should include a combination of negative values, zero, and positive values.

Step 3 Plot the points.

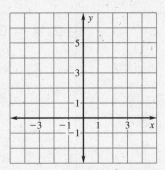

Step 4 Connect the points by drawing a line through them. Use arrows to indicate that the graph goes on without end.

Example 2 *Graph y = b and x = a*

Graph (a) $y = -3$ **and (b)** $x = 2$.

Solution

The equations $y = -3$ and $0x + 1y = -3$ are equivalent. For any value of x, the ordered pair $(x, -3)$ is a solution of $y = -3$.

a. Regardless of the value of x, the value of y is always _____. The graph of $y = -3$ is a _____ line 3 units _____ the x-axis.

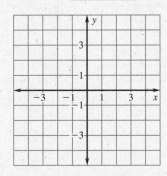

b. Regardless of the value of y, the value of x is always _____. The graph of $x = 2$ is a _____ line 2 units to the _____ of the y-axis.

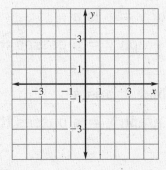

Your Notes

✔ *Checkpoint* **Graph the equation.**

1. $y = 2x - 1$

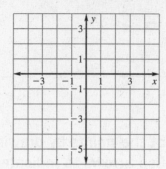

2. $x = 0.5$

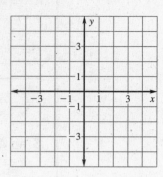

3. $y = -4x + 1$

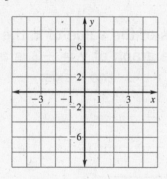

4. $y = -1.5$

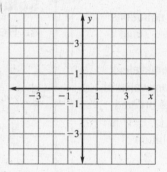

EQUATIONS OF HORIZONTAL AND VERTICAL LINES

1. The graph of $y = b$ is a _____ line.

2. The line of graph $y = b$ passes through the point _____.

3. The graph of $x = a$ is a _____ line.

4. The line of graph $x = a$ passes through the point _____.

 Copyright © McDougal Littell/Houghton Mifflin Company.

Example 3   *Graph a linear function*

Graph the function $y = 2x + 2$ with domain $x \geq 0$. Then identify the range of the function.

Solution

Step 1 Make a _____.

x	0	1	2	3	4
y					

Step 2 Plot the _____.

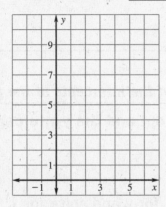

Step 3 Connect the points with a _____ because the domain is _____.

Step 4 Identify the range. From the graph, you can see that all points have a y-coordinate of _____, so the range of the function is _____.

✔ *Checkpoint* **Complete the following exercise.**

5. Graph the function $y = -x + 4$ with domain $x \geq 0$. Then identify the range of the function.

4.3 Graph Using Intercepts

Goal • Graph a linear equation using intercepts.

Your Notes

VOCABULARY
x-intercept
y-intercept

Example 1 *Find the intercepts of the graph of an equation*

Find the *x*-intercept and the *y*-intercept of the graph of $8x - 2y = 32$.

Solution

1. Substitute ___ for *y* and solve for *x*.

$$8x - 2y = 32$$ Write original equation.

$$8x - 2(\underline{}) = 32$$ Substitute ___ for *y*.

$$x = \frac{\boxed{}}{\boxed{}} = \underline{}$$ Solve for ___.

2. Substitute ___ for *x* and solve for *y*.

$$8x - 2y = 32$$ Write original equation.

$$8(\underline{}) - 2y = 32$$ Substitute ___ for *x*.

$$y = \frac{\boxed{}}{\boxed{}} = \underline{}$$ Solve for ___.

The *x*-intercept is ___ . The *y*-intercept is _____ .

Your Notes

✅ *Checkpoint* **Find the *x*-intercept and *y*-intercept of the graph of the equation.**

1. $2x + 3y = 18$	**2.** $-12x - 4y = 36$

Example 2 *Use intercepts to graph an equation*

Graph $3.5x + 2y = 14$. Label the points where the line crosses the axis.

Solution

Step 1 Find the _____.

$3.5x + 2y = 14$	$3.5x + 2y = 14$
$3.5x + 2(\_\_) = 14$	$3.5(\_\_) + 2y = 14$
$x = \dfrac{\boxed{}}{\boxed{}} = \_\_$	$y = \dfrac{\boxed{}}{\boxed{}} = \_\_$

Step 2 Plot the points that correspond to the intercepts.

The *x*-intercept is ___, so plot the point _____.

The *y*-intercept is ___, so plot the point _____.

Step 3 _____ the points by drawing a line through them.

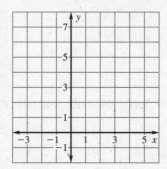

CHECK

You can check the graph of the equation by using a third point. When $x = 2$, $y =$ _____, so the ordered pair _____ is a third solution of the equation. You can see that _____ lies on the graph, so the graph is correct.

Example 3   *Use a graph to find the intercepts*

Identify the *x*-intercept and *y*-intercept of the graph.

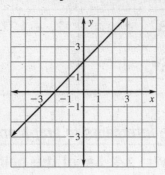

Solution

To find the *x*-intercept, look to see where the graph crosses the _____. The *x*-intercept is _____. To find the *y*-intercept, look to see where the graph crosses the _____. The *y*-intercept is ____.

✓ *Checkpoint* **Complete the following exercises.**

3. Graph $2x - 7y = 14$. Label the points where the line crosses the axes.

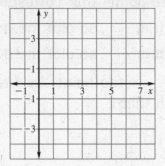

4. Identify the *x*-intercept and *y*-intercept of the graph.

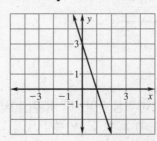

4.4 Find Slope and Rate of Change

Goal • Find the slope of a line and interpret slope as a rate of change.

Your Notes

VOCABULARY

Slope

Rate of change

FINDING THE SLOPE OF A LINE

Words

The slope of the nonvertical line passing through the two points (x_1, y_1) and (x_2, y_2) is the ratio of the _____ (change in y) to the _____ (change in x).

$$\text{slope} = \frac{\boxed{}}{\boxed{}} = \frac{\text{change in } y}{\text{change in } x}$$

Symbols

$$m = \frac{y_2 - y_1}{x_2 - x_1}$$

Graph

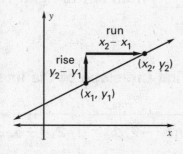

Example 1　*Find a slope*

Find the slope of the line shown.

a. Let $(x_1, y_1) = (-1, 2)$
and $(x_2, y_2) = (3, 5)$.

b. Let $(x_1, y_1) = (1, 4)$
and $(x_2, y_2) = (3, -2)$.

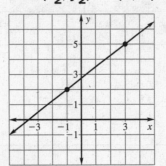　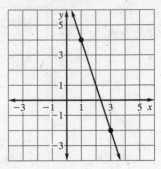

> Keep the *x*- and *y*-coordinates in the same order in the numerator and denominator when calculating slope. This will help avoid error.

Solution

a. $m = \dfrac{y_2 - y_1}{x_2 - x_1}$　　**Write formula for slope.**

$= \dfrac{\boxed{} - 2}{\boxed{} - (-1)}$　　**Substitute.**

$= \dfrac{}{}$　　**Simplify.**

The line _____ from left to right. The slope is

_____ .

b. $m = \dfrac{y_2 - y_1}{x_2 - x_1}$　　**Write formula for slope.**

$= \dfrac{\boxed{} - 4}{\boxed{} - 1}$　　**Substitute.**

$= \dfrac{}{} = \underline{}$　　**Simplify.**

The line _____ from left to right. The slope is

_____ .

✔ *Checkpoint* **Find the slope of the line passing through the points.**

1. $(-3, -1)$ and $(-2, 1)$	**2.** $(-6, 3)$ and $(5, -2)$

Example 2 *Find the slope of a line*

Find the slope of the line shown.

a. Let $(x_1, y_1) = (2, 5)$
and $(x_2, y_2) = (-4, 5)$.

b. Let $(x_1, y_1) = (4, -2)$
and $(x_2, y_2) = (4, 3)$.

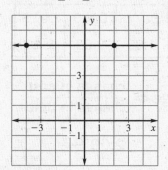
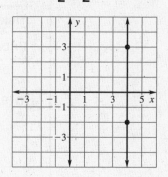

Solution

a. $m = \dfrac{y_2 - y_1}{x_2 - x_1}$ Write formula for slope.

$\quad = \dfrac{5 - \boxed{}}{4 - \boxed{}}$ Substitute.

$\quad = \underline{}$ Simplify.

The line is _____. The slope is _____.

b. $m = \dfrac{y_2 - y_1}{x_2 - x_1}$ Write formula for slope.

$\quad = \dfrac{3 - \boxed{}}{4 - \boxed{}}$ Substitute.

$\quad = \underline{}$ Simplify.

The line is _____. The slope is _____.

✔ *Checkpoint* **Find the slope of the line passing through the points. Then classify the line by its slope.**

3. $(1, -2)$ and $(1, 3)$	**4.** $(-3, 7)$ and $(4, 7)$

Example 3   *Find a rate of change*

Gas Prices The table shows the cost of a gallon of gas for a number of days. Find the rate of change with respect to time.

Time (days)	Day 1	Day 3	Day 5
Price/gal ($)	1.99	2.09	2.19

Rate of change $= \dfrac{\text{change in cost}}{\text{change in time}}$ **Write formula.**

$= \dfrac{2.09 - \boxed{}}{3 - \boxed{}}$ **Substitute.**

$= \dfrac{\boxed{}}{\boxed{}} = \underline{}$ **Simplify.**

The rate of change in price is _____ per day.

✔ *Checkpoint*

5. The table shows the change in temperature over time. Find the rate of change in degrees Fahrenheit with respect to time.

Temperature (°F)	Time (hours)
38	0
43	2
48	4
53	6

Homework

4.5 Graph Using Slope-Intercept Form

Goal • Graph linear equations using slope-intercept form.

Your Notes

VOCABULARY

Slope-intercept form

_____

Parallel

FINDING THE SLOPE AND Y-INTERCEPT OF A LINE

Words

A linear equation of the form $y = mx + b$ is written in

_____

where ____ is the slope and ____ is the y-intercept of the equation's graph.

Graph

Symbols

$y = mx + b$

$y = 2x + 1$

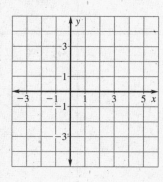

Example 1 *Identify slope and y-intercept*

Identify the slope and *y*-intercept of the line with the given equation.

a. $y = x + 3$ **b.** $-2x + y = 5$

Solution

a. The equation is in the form _____. So, the slope of the line is ___, and the *y*-intercept is ___.

b. Rewrite the equation in slope-intercept form by solving for ___.

$-2x + y = 5$ Write original equation.

$y = $ _____   Subtract _____ from each side.

The line has a slope of ___ and a *y*-intercept of ___.

✓ *Checkpoint* Identify the slope and *y*-intercept of the line with the given equation.

1. $y = 4x - 1$	**2.** $4x - 2y = 8$
3. $4y = 3x + 16$	**4.** $6x + 3y = -21$

Example 2 *Graph an equation using slope-intercept form*

Graph the equation $4x + y = 2$.

Solution

Step 1 Rewrite the equation in slope-intercept form.

_____

Step 2 _____ the slope and the *y*-intercept.

$m =$ ____ $b =$ ___

Step 3 _____ the point that corresponds to the
y-intercept, (_____).

Step 4 Use the slope to locate a second point on the line.
Draw a line through the two points.

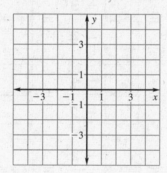

✔ *Checkpoint* **Complete the following exercise.**

5. Graph the equation $-\frac{1}{2}x + y = 1$.

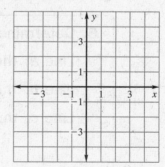

Example 3 *Identify parallel lines*

Determine which of the lines are parallel.

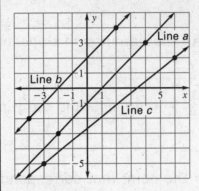

Solution

Find the slope of each line.

Line a: $m = \dfrac{\boxed{} - 3}{\boxed{} - 4} = \dfrac{\boxed{}}{\boxed{}} = \underline{}$

Line b: $m = \dfrac{\boxed{} - 4}{\boxed{} - 2} = \dfrac{\boxed{}}{\boxed{}} = \underline{}$

Line c: $m = \dfrac{\boxed{} - 2}{\boxed{} - 6} = \dfrac{\boxed{}}{\boxed{}} = \underline{}$

Lines ___ and ___ have the same slope. They are parallel.

✔ *Checkpoint* **Complete the following exercise.**

6. Determine which lines are parallel.

   Line a: through $(2, 5)$ and $(-2, 2)$

   Line b: through $(4, 1)$ and $(-3, -4)$

   Line c: through $(2, 3)$ and $(-2, 0)$

Homework

4.6 Model Direct Variation

Goal • Write and graph direct variation equations.

Your Notes

VOCABULARY

Direct variation

Constant of variation

Example 1   *Identify direct variation equations*

Tell whether the equation represents direct variation. If so, identify the constant of variation.

a. $4x + 2y = 0$ **b.** $-2x + y = 3$

Solution

To tell whether an equation represents direct variation, try to rewrite the equation in the form $y = ax$.

a. $4x + 2y = 0$ Write original equation.

$\qquad 2y = $ _____   Subtract _____ from each side.

$\qquad\quad y = $ _____   Simplify.

Because the equation $4x + 2y = 0$ _____ be rewritten in the form $y = ax$, it _____ direct variation. The constant of variation is _____.

b. $-2x + y = 3$ Write original equation.

$\qquad y = $ _____ $+ 3$ Add _____ to each side.

Because the equation $-2x + y = 3$ _____ be rewritten in the form $y = ax$, it _____ direct variation.

Copyright © McDougal Littell/Houghton Mifflin Company.

Lesson 4.6 • **Algebra 1 Notetaking Guide**   **91**

✅ *Checkpoint* **Tell whether the equation represents direct variation. If so, identify the constant of variation.**

1. $3x + 4y = 0$	**2.** $5x + y = 1$

Example 2   *Graph direct variation equations*

Graph the direct variation equation.

a. $y = -5x$ **b.** $y = \dfrac{3}{5}x$

Solution

> The graph of a direct variation equation is a line with a slope of a and a y-intercept of 0. This line passes through the origin.

a. Plot a point at the origin. The slope is equal to the constant of variation, or _____. Find and plot a second point, then draw a line through the points.

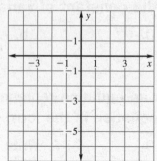

b. Plot a point at the origin. The slope is equal to the constant of variation, or _____. Find and plot a second point, then draw a line through the points.

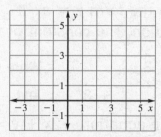

Example 3 *Write and use a direct variation equation*

The graph of a direct variation
equation is shown.

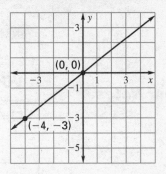

a. Write the direct variation
equation.

b. Find the value of y when
$x = 80$.

Solution

a. Because y varies directly with x, the equation has the
form $y = ax$. Use the fact that $y = -3$ when $x = -4$
to find a.

$y = ax$	Write direct variation equation.
$\underline{\hspace{1cm}} = a(\underline{\hspace{1cm}})$	Substitute.
$\underline{\hspace{1cm}} = a$	Solve for a.

A direct variation equation that relates x and y is

$y = \underline{\hspace{1cm}}$.

b. When $x = 80$, $y = \underline{\hspace{1cm}} = \underline{\hspace{1cm}}$.

✔ **Checkpoint** **Complete the following exercises.**

3. Graph the direct variation equation $y = \dfrac{1}{2}x$.

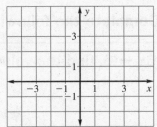

4. The graph of a direct variation equation passes
through the point $(3, -4)$. Write the direct variation
equation and find the value of y when $x = 15$.

4.7 Graph Linear Functions

Goal • Use function notation.

Your Notes

VOCABULARY

Function notation

Family of functions

Parent linear function

Example 1 *Find an x-value*

For the function $f(x) = 3x + 1$, find the value of x so that $f(x) = 10$.

Solution

$f(x) = 3x + 1$	Write original equation.
____ $= 3x + 1$	Substitute ____ for $f(x)$.
____ $= x$	Solve for x.

When $x =$ ___, $f(x) = 10$.

✔ **Checkpoint** Complete the following exercises.

1. For $f(x) = 6x - 6$, find the value of x so that $f(x) = 24$.

---

2. For $f(x) = 7x + 3$, find the value of x so that $f(x) = 17$.

Example 2 *Graph a function*

Text Messages A wireless communication provider estimates that the number of text messages m (in millions) sent over several years can be modeled by the function $m = 120t + 95$ where t represents the number of years since 2002. Graph the function and identify its domain and range.

t	m
0	_____
1	_____
2	_____
3	_____

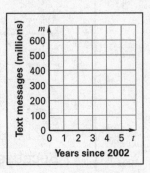

The domain of the function is $t \geq$ ____. From the graph or table, you can see that the range of the function is $m \geq$ ____.

✔ *Checkpoint* **Complete the following exercise.**

3. Use the model from Example 2 to find the value of t so that $m = 1055$. Explain what the solution means in this situation.

PARENT FUNCTION FOR LINEAR FUNCTIONS

1. The _____ is the most basic linear function.

2. _____ is the form of the parent linear function.

Example 3 *Compare graphs with the graph f(x) = x*

Graph the function. Compare the graph with the graph of $f(x) = x$.

a. $p(x) = x - 4$

b. $q(x) = -2x$

Solution

a.

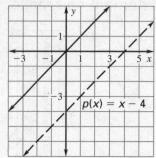

b.

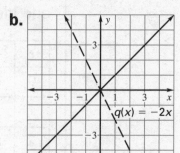

Because the graphs of p and f have the same slope, m = 1, the lines are _____. Also, the y-intercept of the graph of p is ____ less than the y-intercept of the graph of f.

Because the slope of the graph of q _____ from left to right and the slope of the graph of f _____ from left to right, the slope of q is _____. The y-intercept of both graphs is ____.

✔ **Checkpoint** **Complete the following exercise.**

4. Graph $r(x) = \frac{1}{2}x$. Compare the graph with the graph of $f(x) = x$.

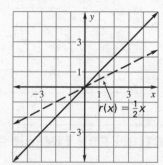

COMPARING GRAPHS OF LINEAR FUNCTIONS WITH THE GRAPH OF $f(x) = x$

$g(x) = x + b$

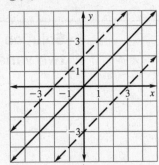

The graphs have the same _____.

The graphs have different _____.

Graphs of this family are _____ of the graph of $f(x) = x$.

$g(x) = mx$ where $m > 0$

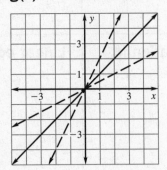

The graphs have different (positive) _____.

The graphs have the same _____.

Graphs of this family are vertical _____ or _____ of the graph of $f(x) = x$.

$g(x) = mx$ where $m < 0$

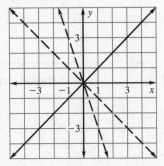

The graphs have different (negative) _____.

The graphs have the same _____.

Graphs of this family are vertical _____ or _____ or _____ of the graph of $f(x) = x$.

Words to Review

Give an example of the vocabulary word.

Quadrant	Solution of an equation in two variables.
Graph of an equation in two variables	Linear equation
Standard form of a linear equation	Linear function
x-intercept	y-intercept
Slope	Rate of change

Slope-intercept form	Parallel
Direct variation	Constant of variation
Function notation	Family of functions
Parent linear function	

Review your notes and Chapter 4 by using the Chapter Review on pages 271–274 of your textbook.

5.1 Write Linear Equations in Slope-Intercept Form

Goal • Write equations of lines.

Your Notes

Example 1 *Use slope and y-intercept to write an equation*

Write an equation of the line with a slope of −4 and a *y*-intercept of 6.

> Use the slope-intercept form ($y = mx + b$) to write an equation of a line if slope and *y*-intercept are given.

Solution

$y = mx + b$ Write slope-intercept form.

$y = \underline{\quad} x + \underline{\quad}$ Substitute _____ for *m* and ___ for *b*.

✓ *Checkpoint* Write an equation of the line with the given slope and *y*-intercept.

1. Slope is 8; *y*-intercept is −5.	**2.** Slope is $\frac{2}{3}$; *y*-intercept is −2.
3. Slope is −3; *y*-intercept is 7.	**4.** Slope is $-\frac{5}{2}$; *y*-intercept is 9.

Example 2 *Write an equation of a line given two points*

Write an equation of the line shown.

Solution

Step 1 Calculate the slope.

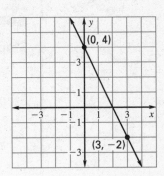

$$m = \frac{y_2 - y_1}{x_2 - x_1}$$

You can write an equation of a line if you know the *y*-intercept and any other point on the line.

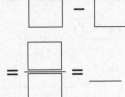

$$= \frac{\boxed{} - \boxed{}}{\boxed{} - \boxed{}}$$

$$= \frac{\boxed{}}{\boxed{}} = \underline{}$$

Step 2 Write an equation of the line. The line crosses the *y*-axis at _____. So, the *y*-intercept is ___.

$y = mx + b$ Write slope-intercept form.

$y = \underline{}x + \underline{}$ Substitute _____ for *m* and
                                    ___ for *b*.

✓ *Checkpoint* **Complete the following exercise.**

5. Write an equation of the line shown.

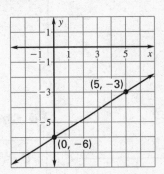

Example 3 *Write a linear function*

Write an equation for the linear function *f* with the values $f(0) = 4$ and $f(2) = 12$.

Solution

Step 1 Write $f(0) = 4$ as _____ and $f(2) = 12$ as

_____.

Step 2 Calculate the slope of the line that passes through _____ and _____.

$$m = \frac{y_2 - y_1}{x_2 - x_1}$$

$$= \frac{\boxed{} - \boxed{}}{\boxed{} - \boxed{}}$$

$$= \frac{\boxed{}}{\boxed{}}$$

$$= \underline{}$$

Step 3 Write an equation of the line. The line crosses the *y*-axis at (0, ___). So, the *y*-intercept is ___.

$y = mx + b$ Write slope-intercept form.

$y = \underline{}$ Substitute ___ for *m* and ___ for *b*.

The function is _____.

✔ *Checkpoint* **Complete the following exercise.**

Homework

6. Write an equation for the linear function with the values $f(0) = 3$ and $f(3) = 15$.

5.2 Use Linear Equations in Slope-Intercept Form

Goal • Write an equation of a line using points on the line.

Your Notes

WRITING AN EQUATION OF A LINE IN SLOPE-INTERCEPT FORM

Step 1 **Identify** the slope ____. You can use the _____ _____ to calculate the slope if you know two points on the line.

Step 2 **Find** the _____. You can substitute the _____ and the _____ of a point (x, y) on the line into $y = mx + b$. Then solve for ___.

Step 3 **Write** an equation using _____.

Example 1 *Write an equation given the slope and a point*

Write an equation of the line that passes through the point (1, 2) and has a slope of 3.

Solution

Step 1 **Identify** the slope. The slope is ___.

Step 2 **Find** the y-intercept. Substitute the slope and the coordinates of the given point into $y = mx + b$. Solve for b.

> Be careful not to mix up the x- and y-values when you substitute.

$y = mx + b$ Write slope-intercept form.

___ = ___(___) + b   Substitute ___ for m, ___ for x, and ___ for y.

_____ = b   Solve for ___.

Step 3 **Write** an equation of the line.

$y = mx + b$ Write slope-intercept form.

$y =$ _____   Substitute ___ for m and _____ for b.

✔ Checkpoint Complete the following exercise.

1. Write an equation of the line that passes through the point (2, 2) and has a slope of 4.

Example 2 *Write an equation given two points*

Write an equation of the line that passes through (2, −3) and (−2, 1).

Solution

Step 1 Calculate the slope.

$$m = \frac{y_2 - y_1}{x_2 - x_1}$$

$$= \frac{\boxed{} - \boxed{}}{\boxed{} - \boxed{}}$$

$$= \frac{\boxed{}}{\boxed{}} = \underline{}$$

> You can also find the y-intercept using the coordinates of the other given point.

Step 2 Find the y-intercept. Use the slope and the point (2, −3).

$$y = mx + b$$ Write slope-intercept form.

$$-3 = \underline{}(\underline{}) + b$$ Substitute ____ for *m*, ____ for *x*, and ____ for *y*.

$$\underline{} = b$$ Solve for *b*.

Step 3 Write an equation of the line.

$$y = mx + b$$ Write slope-intercept form.

$$y = \underline{}$$ Substitute ____ for *m* and ____ for *b*.

✓ Checkpoint Complete the following exercise.

2. Write an equation for the line that passes through $(-8, -13)$ and $(4, 2)$.

---

3. Write an equation for the line that passes through $(-3, 4)$ and $(1, -2)$.

HOW TO WRITE EQUATIONS IN SLOPE-INTERCEPT FORM

1. Given slope m and y-intercept b.

   Substitute ____ and ____ in the equation _____.

2. Given slope m and one point.

   Substitute ____ and the _____ of the point in _____. Solve for ____. Write the _____.

3. Given two points.

   Use the points to find the slope ____. Then substitute ____ and the _____ of _____ _____ in _____. Solve for ____. Write the _____.

Homework

5.3 Write Linear Equations in Point-Slope Form

Goal • Write linear equations in point-slope form.

VOCABULARY

Point-slope form

POINT-SLOPE FORM

The **point-slope form** of the equation of the nonvertical line through a given point (x_1, y_1) with a slope of m is

_____.

Example 1 *Write an equation in point-slope form*

Write an equation in point-slope form on the line that passes through the point (3, 2) and has a slope of 2.

Solution

$y - y_1 = m(x - x_1)$ Write point-slope form.

$y -$ ___ $=$ ___ $(x -$ ___$)$ Substitute ___ for m, ___ for x_1, and ___ for y_1.

Example 2   *Graph an equation in point-slope form*

Graph the equation $y - 2 = \frac{1}{2}(x - 2)$.

Solution

Because the equation is in point-slope form, you know
that the line has a slope of ____ and passes through the
point _____.

Plot the point _____ Find a second point on the line
using the _____. Draw a line through the points.

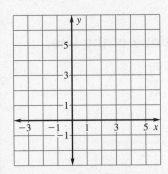

✓ *Checkpoint* **Complete the following exercises.**

1. Write an equation in point-slope form of the line
   that passes through the point $(-3, 5)$ and has a
   slope of 4.

2. Graph the equation $y + 1 = 2(x - 1)$.

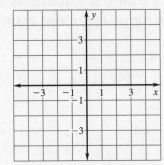

Example 3 *Use point-slope form to write an equation*

Write an equation in point-slope form of the line shown.

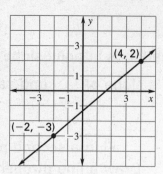

Solution

Step 1 **Find** the slope of the line.

$$m = \frac{y_2 - y_1}{x_2 - x_1}$$

$$= \frac{\boxed{} - \boxed{}}{\boxed{} - \boxed{}}$$

$$= \frac{\boxed{}}{\boxed{}} = \underline{}$$

Step 2 **Write** the equation in point-slope form.
You can use either given point.

Method 1 Use $(-2, -3)$.   **Method 2** Use $(4, 2)$.

$y - y_1 = m(x - x_1)$ $y - y_1 = m(x - x_1)$

_____   _____

CHECK Check that the equations are equivalent by writing them in slope-intercept form.

$y \underline{} = \underline{} x \underline{}$ $y \underline{} = \underline{} x \underline{}$

$y = \underline{}$ $y = \underline{}$

Homework

5.4 Write Linear Equations in Standard Form

Goal • Write equations in standard form.

Example 1 *Write equivalent equations in standard form*

Write two equations in standard form that are equivalent to $4x + 2y = 12$.

Solution

To write one equivalent equation, multiply each side by _____.

_____

To write one equivalent equation, multiply each side by ___.

_____

✔ **Checkpoint** Complete the following exercises.

1. Write two equations in standard form that are equivalent to $6x - 4y = 6$.

2. Write two equations in standard form that are equivalent to $-12x + 6y = -9$.

Example 2   *Write an equation from a graph*

Write an equation in standard form of the line shown.

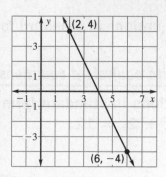

Solution

Step 1 Calculate the slope.

$$m = \frac{y_2 - y_1}{x_2 - x_1}$$

$$= \frac{\boxed{} - \boxed{}}{\boxed{} - \boxed{}}$$

$$= \frac{\boxed{}}{\boxed{}}$$

$$= \underline{}$$

Step 2 Write an equation in point-slope form. Use (2, 4).

$y - y_1 = m(x - x_1)$ **Write point-slope form.**

$y - \underline{} = \underline{}(x - \underline{})$ **Substitute ___ for y_1, _____ for m, and ___ for x_1.**

Step 3 Rewrite the equation in standard form.

$y - \underline{} = \underline{}x + \underline{}$ **Distributive property**

$y + \underline{}x = \underline{}$ **Collect variable terms on one side, constants on the other.**

Your Notes

3. Write an equation in standard form of the line through (3, −1) and (2, −4).

Example 3 *Write an equation of a line*

Write an equation of the specified line.

a. Line *A*

b. Line *B*

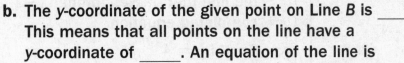

Solution

a. The *x*-coordinate of the given point on Line *A* is _____. This means that all points on the line have an *x*-coordinate of _____. An equation of the line is _____.

b. The *y*-coordinate of the given point on Line *B* is _____. This means that all points on the line have a *y*-coordinate of _____. An equation of the line is _____.

Example 4 *Complete an equation in standard form*

Find the missing coefficient in the equation of the line shown. Write the completed equation.

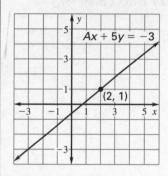

$Ax + 5y = -3$

(2, 1)

Solution

Step 1 Find the value of A. Substitute the coordinates of the given point for x and y in the equation.

$Ax + 5y = -3$	**Write equation.**
$A(\underline{\quad}) + 5(\underline{\quad}) = -3$	**Substitute** $\underline{\quad}$ **for** x **and** $\underline{\quad}$ **for** y.
$\underline{\quad}A + \underline{\quad} = -3$	**Simplify.**
$\underline{\quad}A = \underline{\quad}$	**Subtract** $\underline{\quad}$ **from each side.**
$A = \underline{\quad}$	**Divide by** $\underline{\quad}$.

Step 2 Complete the equation.

$\underline{\quad}x + 5y = -3$ **Substitute** $\underline{\quad}$ **for** A.

✔ *Checkpoint* **Complete the following exercises.**

4. Write equations of the horizontal and vertical lines that pass through $(-10, 5)$.

Homework

5. Find the missing coefficient in the equation of the line that passes through $(-2, 2)$. Write the completed equation.

$6x + By = 4$

5.5 Write Equations of Parallel and Perpendicular Lines

Goal • Write equations of parallel and perpendicular lines.

Your Notes

VOCABULARY

Converse

_____

Perpendicular lines

PARALLEL LINES

If two nonvertical lines have the same _____, then they are _____.

If two nonvertical lines are _____, then they have the same _____.

Example 1 *Write an equation of a parallel line*

Write an equation of the line that passes through (2, 4) and is parallel to the line $y = 4x + 1$.

Solution

Step 1 Identify the slope. The graph of the given equation has a slope of ___. So, the parallel line through (2, 4) has a slope of ___.

Step 2 Find the y-intercept. Use the slope and the given point.

$y = mx + b$	Write slope-intercept form.
___ = ___(___) + b	Substitute ___ for m, ___ for x, and ___ for y.
_____ = b	Solve for b.

Step 3 Write an equation. Use $y = mx + b$.

$y =$ _____	Substitute ___ for m and _____ for b.

Your Notes

PERPENDICULAR LINES

If two nonvertical lines have the slopes that
are _____, then the lines
are _____.

If two nonvertical lines are _____, then their
slopes are _____.

Example 2 *Determine parallel or perpendicular lines*

Determine which of the following lines, if any, are
parallel or perpendicular:

Line *a:* $12x - 3y = 3$

Line *b:* $y = 4x + 2$

Line *c:* $4y + x = 8$

Solution

Find the slopes of the lines.

Line *b*: The equation is in slope-intercept form.
The slope is ___.

Write the equations for lines *a* and *c* in
slope-intercept form.

Line *a*: $12x - 3y = 3$

$$-3y = \underline{\hspace{1cm}} + 3$$

$$y = \underline{\hspace{1cm}}$$

Line *c*: $4y + x = 8$

$$4y = \underline{\hspace{1cm}} + 8$$

$$y = \underline{\hspace{1cm}}$$

Lines *a* and *b* have a slope of ___, so they are _____.

Line *c* has a slope of _____, the negative reciprocal

of ___, so it is _____ to lines *a* and *b*.

✔ *Checkpoint* **Complete the following exercises.**

1. Write an equation of the line that passes through $(-4, 6)$ and is parallel to the line $y = -3x + 2$.

2. Determine which of the following lines, if any, are parallel or perpendicular.

   Line *a:* $4x + y = 2$

   Line *b:* $5y + 20x = 10$

   Line *c:* $8y = 2x + 8$

Example 3   *Determine whether lines are perpendicular*

Determine if the following lines are perpendicular.

Line *a:* $6y = 5x + 8$

Line *b:* $-10y = 12x + 10$

Solution

Find the slopes of the lines. Write the equations in slope-intercept form.

Line *a:* $6y = 5x + 8$

$$y = \underline{\hspace{3cm}}$$

Line *b:* $-10y = 12x + 10$

$$y = \underline{\hspace{3cm}}$$

The slope of line *a* is ____. The slope of line *b* is ____.

The two slopes _____ negative reciprocals, so lines *a* and *b* _____ perpendicular.

Example 4 *Write an equation of a perpendicular line*

Write an equation of the line that passes through $(-3, 4)$ and is perpendicular to the line $y = \frac{1}{3}x + 2$.

Solution

Step 1 Identify the slope. The graph of the given equation has a slope of ____. Because the slopes of perpendicular lines are negative reciprocals, the slope of the perpendicular line through $(-3, 4)$ is _____.

Step 2 Find the y-intercept. Use the slope and the given point.

$y = mx + b$	Write slope-intercept form.
___ = _____ (___) + b	Substitute _____ for m, _____ for x, and ___ for y.
_____ = b	Solve for b.

Step 3 Write an equation.

$y = mx + b$	Write slope-intercept form.
$y = $ _____	Substitute _____ for m and _____ for b.

✔ *Checkpoint* **Complete the following exercises.**

3. Determine whether line a through $(1, 3)$ and $(3, 4)$ is perpendicular to line b through $(1, -3)$ and $(2, -5)$. Justify your answer using slopes.

Homework

4. Write an equation of the line that passes through $(4, -2)$ and is perpendicular to the line $y = 5x + 2$.

5.6 Fit a Line to Data

Goal • Make scatter plots and write equations to model data.

Your Notes

VOCABULARY

Scatter plot

Correlation

Line of fit

CORRELATION

- If *y* tends to increase as *x* increases, the paired data are said to have a _____ correlation.

- If *y* tends to decrease as *x* increases, the paired data are said to have a _____ correlation.

- If *x* and *y* have no apparent relationship, the paired data are said to have _____ correlation.

Example 1 *Describe the correlation of data*

Describe the correlation of data graphed in the scatter plot.

a.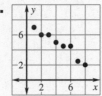

b.

Solution

a. _____   b. _____
   correlation   correlation

Example 2 *Make a scatter plot*

a. Make a scatter plot of the data in the table.

x	1	1.5	2	2	3	3.5	4
y	3	1	1	−0.5	−1	−0.5	−2

b. Describe the correlation of the data.

Solution

a. Treat the data as ordered pairs. Plot the ordered pairs as _____ in a coordinate plane.

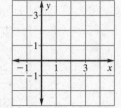

b. The scatter plot shows a _____ correlation.

USING A LINE OF FIT TO MODEL DATA

Step 1 **Make** a _____ of the data.

Step 2 **Decide** whether the data can be modeled by a _____.

Step 3 **Draw** a line that appears to ____ the data closely. There should be approximately as many points _____ the line as _____ it.

Step 4 **Write** an equation using _____ points on the line. The points do not have to represent actual data pairs, but they must lie on the line of fit.

Example 3 *Write an equation to model data*

Game Attendance The table shows the average attendance at a school's varsity basketball games for various years. Write an equation that models the average attendance at varsity basketball games as a function of the number of years since 2000.

Year	2000	2001	2002	2003	2004	2005	2006
Avg. Game Attendance	488	497	525	567	583	621	688

Solution

Step 1 **Make** a _____ of the data. Let x represent the number of years since 2000. Let y represent average game attendance.

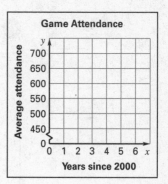

Step 2 **Decide** whether the data can be modeled by a line. Because the scatter plot shows a _____ correlation, you can fit a line to the data.

Step 3 **Draw** a line that appears to fit the points in the scatter plot _____.

Step 4 **Write** an equation using two points on the line. Use (1, 493) and (5, 621).

Find the _____ of the line.

$$m = \frac{y_2 - y_1}{x_2 - x_1} = \frac{\boxed{} - \boxed{}}{\boxed{} - \boxed{}}$$

$$= \frac{\boxed{}}{\boxed{}}$$

$$= \boxed{}$$

Find the y-intercept of the line. Use the point (5, 621).

$y = mx + b$ **Write slope-intercept form.**

_____ = ____(___) + b   **Substitute _____ for _m_, ____
for _x_, and _____ for _y_.**

_____ = b   **Solve for _b_.**

An equation of the line of fit is _____ .

The average attendance _y_ of varsity basketball games
can be modeled by the function _____ where
_x_ is the number of years since 2000.

✔ *Checkpoint* **Complete the following exercises.**

1. Make a scatter plot of the data in the table. Describe
   the correlation of the data.

x	1	2	2	3	4	5
y	5	5	6	7	8	8

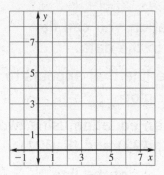

2. Use the data in the table to write an equation that
   models _y_ as a function of _x_.

x	1	2	3	4	5	6
y	65	76	82	86	92	97

5.7 Predict with Linear Models

Goal • Make predictions using best-fitting lines.

Your Notes

VOCABULARY

Best-fitting line

Interpolation

Extrapolation

Zero of a function

Example 1 *Interpolate using an equation*

NFL Salaries The table shows the average National Football League (NFL) player's salary (in thousands of dollars) from 1997 to 2001.

Year	1997	1999	2000	2001
Average Player's Salary (in thousands of dollars)	585	708	787	986

a. Make a scatter plot of the data.

b. Find an equation that models the average NFL player's salary (in thousands of dollars) as a function of the number of years since 1997.

c. Approximate the average NFL player's salary in 1998.

Solution

a. Enter the data into lists on a graphing calculator. Make a scatter plot, letting the number of years since 1997 be the _____ (0, 2, 3, 4) and the average player's salary be the _____.

b. Perform _____ using the paired data. The equation of the best-fitting line is $y =$ _____.

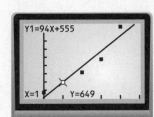

c. Graph the best-fitting line. Use the trace feature and the arrow keys to find the value of the equation when $x =$ ___.

The average NFL player's salary in 1998 was _____ thousand dollars.

Example 2 *Extrapolate using an equation*

NFL Salaries Look back at Example 1.

a. Use the equation from Example 1 to approximate the average NFL player's salary in 2002 and 2003.

b. In 2002, the average NFL player's salary was actually 1180 thousand dollars. In 2003, the average NFL player's salary was actually 1259 thousand dollars. Describe the accuracy of the extrapolations made in part (a).

Solution

a. Evaluate the equation of the best-fitting line from Example 1 for $x =$ ___ and $x =$ ___.

> Y₁(5)
>   1025
> Y₁(6)
>   1119

The model predicts the average NFL player's salary as _____ thousand dollars in 2002 and _____ thousand dollars in 2003.

b. The differences between the predicted average NFL player's salary and the actual average NFL player's salary in 2002 and 2003 are _____ thousand dollars and _____ thousand dollars, respectively. The equation of the best-fitting line gives a less accurate prediction for the years outside of the given years.

RELATING SOLUTIONS OF EQUATIONS, ZEROS OF FUNCTIONS, AND *x*-INTERCEPTS OF GRAPHS

In Chapter 3, you learned to solve an equation like	In Chapter 4, you found the _____ of the graph of a function like	Now you are finding the zero of a function like
$4x - 4 = 0$:	$y = 4x - 4$:	$f(x) = 4x - 4$:
$4x - 4 = 0$		$f(x) = 0$
$4x =$ ___		_____ $= 0$
$x =$ ___		$x =$ ___
The solution of $4x - 4 = 0$ is ___.		The zero of $f(x) = 4x - 4$ is ___.

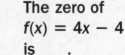

Example 3 *Find the zero of a function*

Public Transit The percentage *y* of people in the U.S. that use public transit to commute to work can be modeled by the function $y = -0.045x + 5.7$ where *x* is the number of years since 1983. Find the zero of the function. Explain what the zero means in this situation.

Solution

Substitute ____ for *y* in the equation of the _____ ____ and solve for *x*.

$y = -0.045x + 5.7$ **Write the equation.**

____ $= -0.045x + 5.7$ **Substitute ____ for *y*.**

_____   **Solve for *x*.**

The zero of the function is about ____. The function has a _____ slope, which means that the percentage of people using public transit to commute to work is _____. According to the model there will be no people who use public transit to commute to work ____ years after ____, or in ____.

✔ *Checkpoint* **Complete the following exercise.**

1. **Baseball Salaries** The table shows the average major league baseball player's salary (in thousands of dollars) from 1997 to 2001.

Year	1997	1999	2000	2001
Average Player's Salary (in thousands of dollars)	1337	1607	1896	2139

Find an equation that models the average major league baseball player's salary (in thousands of dollars) as a function of the number of years since 1997. Approximate the average major league baseball player's salary is 1998, 2002, and 2003.

Homework

Words to Review

Give an example of the vocabulary word.

Point-slope form	Converse
Perpendicular lines	**Scatter plot**
Correlation	**Line of fit**
Best-fitting line	**Interpolation**

Extrapolation	Zero of a function

Review your notes and Chapter 5 by using the Chapter Review on pages 345–348 of your textbook.

6.1 Solve Inequalities Using Addition and Subtraction

Goal • Solve inequalities using addition and subtraction.

Your Notes

VOCABULARY

Graph of a linear inequality in one variable

_____

Equivalent inequalities

Example 1 *Write and graph an inequality*

Food Drive Your school wants to collect at least 5000 pounds of food for a food drive. Write and graph an inequality to describe the amount of food that your school hopes to collect.

Solution

Let p represent the _____

_____. The value of p must

be _____ 5000 pounds. So, an

inequality is _____.

> Remember to use an open circle for < or > and a closed circle for ≤ or ≥.

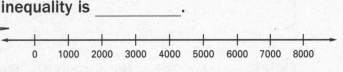

```
<-+----+----+----+----+----+----+----+----+->
  0   1000 2000 3000 4000 5000 6000 7000 8000
```

✓ *Checkpoint* **Complete the following exercise.**

---

1. You must be 16 years old or older to get your driver's license. Write and graph an inequality to describe the ages of people who may get their driver's license.

```
<-+----+----+----+----+----+----+----+----+->
  13   14   15   16   17   18   19   20   21
```

ADDITION PROPERTY OF INEQUALITY

Words Adding the same number to each side of
an inequality produces an _____
_____.

Algebra If $a > b$, then $a + c >$ _____.

If $a < b$, then $a + c <$ _____.

If $a \geq b$, then $a + c \geq$ _____.

If $a \leq b$, then $a + c \leq$ _____.

Example 2 *Solve an inequality using addition*

Solve $n - 3.5 < 2.5$. Graph your solution.

Solution

$n - 3.5 < 2.5$ Write original inequality.

$n - 3.5 +$ _____ $< 2.5 +$ _____   Add _____ to each side.

_____   Simplify.

The solutions are all real numbers _____. Check
by substituting a number _____ for n in the
original inequality.

✔ **Checkpoint** **Solve the inequality. Graph your solution.**

2. $6 > y - 3.3$	3. $z - 7 \geq 4$

SUBTRACTION PROPERTY OF INEQUALITY

Words   Subtracting the same number from each side of an inequality produces an _____ _____.

Algebra   If $a > b$, then $a - c >$ _____.

If $a < b$, then $a - c <$ _____.

If $a \geq b$, then $a - c \geq$ _____.

If $a \leq b$, then $a - c \leq$ _____.

Example 3   *Solve an inequality using subtraction*

Solve $3 \leq y + 8$. Graph your solution.

Solution

$$3 \leq y + 8 \qquad \text{Write original inequality.}$$

$$3 - \underline{\quad} \leq y + 8 - \underline{\quad} \qquad \text{Subtract } \underline{\quad} \text{ from each side.}$$

$$\underline{\qquad\qquad} \qquad \text{Simplify.}$$

You can rewrite _____ as _____. The solutions are all real numbers _____.

✔ Checkpoint Solve the inequality. Graph your solution.

4. $r + 3\frac{1}{4} < 5$	**5.** $3 + m \geq 7.2$

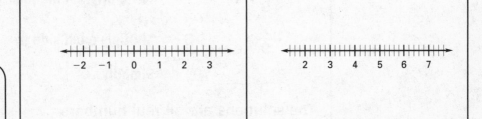

Homework

6.2 Solve Inequalities Using Multiplication and Division

Goal • Solve inequalities using multiplication and division.

MULTIPLICATION PROPERTY OF INEQUALITY

Words Multiplying each side of an inequality by a _____ number produces an

_____.

Multiplying each side of an inequality by a _____ number and _____

_____ produces an equivalent inequality.

Algebra If $a < b$ and $c > 0$, then _____.

If $a < b$ and $c < 0$, then _____.

If $a > b$ and $c > 0$, then _____.

If $a > b$ and $c < 0$, then _____.

This property is also true for inequalities involving $\leq$ and $\geq$.

Example 1 *Solve an inequality using multiplication*

Solve $\frac{y}{9} > 3$. **Graph your solution.**

Solution

$\frac{y}{9} > 3$ Write original inequality.

$\underline{\quad} \cdot \frac{y}{9} > \underline{\quad} \cdot 3$ Multiply each side by ___.

$\underline{\qquad\qquad}$ Simplify.

The solutions are all real numbers _____.

24　25　26　27　28　29　30　31　32

Your Notes

Example 2 *Solve an inequality using multiplication*

Solve $\dfrac{m}{-2} < 5$. Graph your solution.

Solution

$\dfrac{m}{-2} < 5$ Write original inequality.

_____ $\cdot \dfrac{m}{-2} >$ _____ $\cdot 5$ Multiply each side by _____ and _____ the inequality symbol.

_____   Simplify.

The solutions are all real numbers _____.

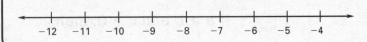

✓ *Checkpoint* **Solve the inequality. Graph your solution.**

1. $\dfrac{r}{7} \le 6$ 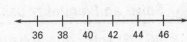	**2.** $\dfrac{s}{-4} > 0.4$ 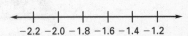
3. $\dfrac{n}{-5} \ge -2$ 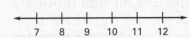	**4.** $\dfrac{w}{6} < -0.8$

DIVISION PROPERTY OF INEQUALITY

Words Dividing each side of an inequality by a _____ number produces an

_____ .

Dividing each side of an inequality by a _____ number and _____

_____

produces an equivalent inequality.

Algebra If $a < b$ and $c > 0$, then _____ .

If $a < b$ and $c < 0$, then _____ .

If $a > b$ and $c > 0$, then _____ .

If $a > b$ and $c < 0$, then _____ .

This property is also true for inequalities involving $\leq$ and $\geq$.

Example 3 *Solve an inequality using division*

Solve $-4x < 36$. Graph your solution.

Solution

$-4x < 36$ Write original inequality.

$\dfrac{-4x}{\boxed{}} > \dfrac{36}{\boxed{}}$ Divide each side by _____ and _____ the inequality symbol.

_____ Simplify.

The solutions are all real numbers _____ .

$$\leftarrow \!\!\!\! \overset{\displaystyle |}{\underset{-13}{}} \ \overset{\displaystyle |}{\underset{-12}{}} \ \overset{\displaystyle |}{\underset{-11}{}} \ \overset{\displaystyle |}{\underset{-10}{}} \ \overset{\displaystyle |}{\underset{-9}{}} \ \overset{\displaystyle |}{\underset{-8}{}} \ \overset{\displaystyle |}{\underset{-7}{}} \ \overset{\displaystyle |}{\underset{-6}{}} \ \overset{\displaystyle |}{\underset{-5}{}} \!\!\!\! \rightarrow$$

Example 4   *Solve a real-world problem*

Pizza Party You have a budget of $45 to buy pizza for a student council meeting. Pizzas cost $7.50 each. Write and solve an inequality to find the possible numbers of pizzas that you can buy.

Solution

Price per pizza (dollars per pizza)	·	Number of pizzas (pizzas)	≤	Budget amount (dollars)

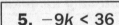   · p ≤   _____

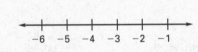   **Write inequality.**

$p \leq$ ___   **Divide each side by _____.**

You can buy at most ___ pizzas.

✔ *Checkpoint* **Solve the inequality. Graph your solution.**

5. $-9k < 36$	**6.** $10n \geq 140$
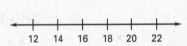	

7. In Example 4, suppose that you had a budget of $50 and each pizza costs $8. Write and solve an inequality to find the possible numbers of pizzas that you can buy.

6.3 Solve Multi-Step Inequalities

Goal • Solve multi-step inequalities.

Your Notes

Example 1 *Solve a two-step inequality*

Solve $4x + 6 \geq 54$. Graph your solution.

Solution

$4x + 6 \geq 54$ Write original inequality.

$4x \geq 48$ Subtract ____ from each side.

_____   Divide each side by ___.

The solutions are all real numbers _____

_____.

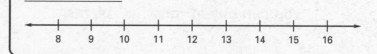

Example 2 *Solve a multi-step inequality*

Solve $-\frac{1}{3}(x + 21) < 2$.

Solution

$-\frac{1}{3}(x + 21) < 2$ Write original inequality.

$-\frac{1}{3}x - \underline{} < 2$ Distributive property

$-\frac{1}{3}x < \underline{}$ Add ____ to each side.

_____   Multiply each side by _____.
                                _____ the inequality symbol.

The solutions are all real numbers _____.

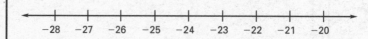

Your Notes

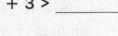✓ **Checkpoint** Solve the inequality. Graph your solution.

1. $-5w - 2 \geq 23$	**2.** $2(y - 2.2) > 0$
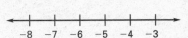	

Example 3   *Identify the number of solutions of an inequality*

Solve the inequality, if possible.

a. $8x + 3 > 2(4x + 1)$

b. $3(8b - 1) \leq 24b - 4$

Solution

a. $8x + 3 > 2(4x + 1)$ **Write original inequality.**

    $8x + 3 >$ _____   **Distributive property**

    _____   **Subtract _____ from each side.**

_____ are solutions because _____

is _____.

b. $3(8b - 1) \leq 24b - 4$ **Write original inequality.**

    _____ $\leq 24b - 4$ **Distributive property**

    _____   **Subtract _____ from each side.**

There are _____ because _____

is _____.

✓ **Checkpoint** Solve the inequality, if possible.

3. $18 + 4w \geq \frac{1}{2}(8w + 36)$	**4.** $-2(3z - 1) < 1 - 6z$

Example 4 *Solve a multi-step problem*

Cell Phone Your cell phone plan is $35 a month for 1000 minutes. You are charged $.25 per minute for any additional minutes. What are the possible numbers of additional minutes you can use if you want to spend no more than $50 on your monthly cell phone bill?

Solution

The amount spent on the monthly plan plus additional minutes must be less than or equal to your monthly budget. Let m be the number of additional minutes that you use.

Price per minute (dollars/min)	·	Number of minutes (minutes)	+	Monthly fee (dollars)	≤	Monthly budget (dollars)

_____ · m + _____ ≤ _____

_____ ≤ _____ Write inequality.

_____ $m \leq$ _____ Subtract _____ from each side.

$m \leq$ _____ Divide each side by _____ .

You can use an additional _____ per month to keep within your monthly cell phone budget.

Solve Compound Inequalities

Goal • Solve and graph compound inequalities.

Your Notes

VOCABULARY

Compound inequality

Example 1 | *Write and graph compound inequalities*

Translate the verbal phrase into an inequality. Then graph the inequality.

a. All real numbers that are greater than or equal to −2 *and* less than 2.

b. All real numbers that are less than or equal to 3 *or* greater than 6.

c. All real numbers that are greater than −8 *and* less than or equal to −3.

Solution

a. −2 ___ *x* ___ 2

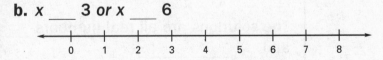

b. *x* ___ 3 *or x* ___ 6

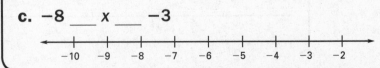

c. −8 ___ *x* ___ −3

Example 2 **Solve a compound inequality with and**

Solve $15 \leq 3x - 3 < 24$. Graph your solution.

Solution

Separate the compound inequality into two inequalities. Then solve each inequality separately.

$15 \leq 3x - 3$ and $3x - 3 < 24$	Write two inequalities.
_____ $\leq 3x$ and $3x <$ _____	Add _____ to each expression.
_____ $\leq x$ and $x <$ _____	Divide each expression by _____.

The compound inequality can be written as _____.
The solutions are all real numbers _____
_____ and _____.

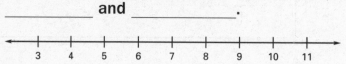

Example 3 **Solve a compound inequality with and**

Solve $15 < -7x + 1 < 50$. Graph your solution.

Solution

$15 < -7x + 1 < 50$	Write original inequality.
_____ $< -7x <$ _____	Subtract _____ from each expression.
_____ $> x >$ _____	Divide each expression by _____ and _____ _____ _____.

The solutions are all real numbers _____
and _____.

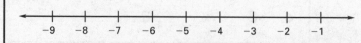

Example 4 *Solve a compound inequality with or*

Solve **5x + 6 ≤ −9 or 2x − 8 > 12. Graph your solution.**

Solution

5x + 6 ≤ −9	*or* 2x − 8 > 12	Write original inequality.
5x ≤ _____	*or* 2x > _____	Use addition or subtraction property of inequality.
x ≤ _____	*or* x > _____	Use division property of inequality.

The solutions are all real numbers _____

_____ or _____.

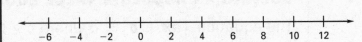

✔ *Checkpoint* **Solve the inequality. Graph your solution.**

1. −3 ≤ −2x + 1 < 11

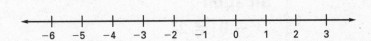

---

2. 9x + 1 < −17 or 7x − 12 > 9

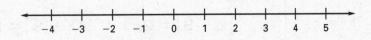

Homework

6.5 Solve Absolute Value Equations

Goal • Solve absolute value equations.

Your Notes

VOCABULARY

Absolute value equation

Absolute deviation

SOLVING AN ABSOLUTE VALUE EQUATION

The equation $|ax + b| = c$ where $c \geq 0$ is equivalent to the statement _____ *or* _____ .

Example 1 *Solve an absolute value equation*

Solve $|x - 9| = 2$.

Solution

$|x - 9| = 2$		Write original equation.
$x - 9 = 2$	*or* $x - 9 = -2$	Rewrite as two equations.
$x = $ ____	*or* $x = $ ____	Add ____ to each side.

The solutions are ____ and ____ . Check your solution.

CHECK

$|x - 9| = 2$	$|x - 9| = 2$	Write original equation.
$|$____$ - 9| = 2$	$|$____$ - 9| = 2$	Substitute for x.
$|$____$| = 2$	$|$____$| = 2$	Subtract.
_____ ✓	_____ ✓	Simplify. Solution checks.

Example 2   *Rewrite an absolute value equation*

Solve $4\left|2x + 8\right| + 6 = 30$.

Solution

First, rewrite the equation in the form _____.

$4\left|2x + 8\right| + 6 = 30$	**Write original equation.**
$4\left|2x + 8\right| = $ _____	**Subtract ___ from each side.**
$\left|2x + 8\right| = $ ___	**Divide each side by ___.**

Next, solve the absolute value equation.

$\left|2x + 8\right| = $ ___	**Write absolute value equation.**
$2x + 8 = $ ___ *or* $2x + 8 = $ _____	**Rewrite as two equations.**
$2x = $ _____ *or* $2x = $ _____	**Subtract ___ from each side.**
$x = $ _____ *or* $x = $ _____	**Divide each side by ___.**

> Remember to check your solutions in the original equation for accuracy.

✔ *Checkpoint* Solve the equation.

1. $\left|x + 6\right| = 11$	2. $3\left|5x - 10\right| + 6 = 21$

Example 3 *Decide if an equation has no solutions*

Solve $|7x - 3| + 8 = 5$, if possible.

Solution

$|7x - 3| + 8 = 5$ Write original equation.

$\quad\quad |7x - 3| =$ _____   Subtract ___ from each side.

The absolute value of a number is never _____. So, there are no solutions.

Example 4 *Use absolute deviation*

The absolute deviation of x from 10 is 1.8. Find the values of x that satisfy this requirement.

Solution

$$\text{Absolute deviation} = |x - \text{given value}|$$

$$\underline{\hspace{3em}} \quad\quad = |x - \underline{\hspace{2em}}|$$

_____   Write original equation.

_____ $= x -$ _____ *or* _____ $= x -$ _____   Rewrite as two equations.

_____ $= x$ *or*   _____ $= x$ Add ____ to each side.

So, x is _____ or _____.

✔ *Checkpoint* **Complete the following exercise.**

3. Find the values of x that satisfy the definition of absolute value for a given value of -13.6 and an absolute deviation of 2.8.

6.6 Solve Absolute Value Inequalities

Goal • Solve absolute value inequalities.

Example 1 *Solve an absolute value inequality*

Solve the inequality. Graph your solution.

a. $|x| \leq 9$ b. $|x| > \frac{1}{4}$

Solution

a. The distance between x and 0 is less than or equal to 9. So, _____ $\leq x \leq$ ___. The solutions are all real numbers _____ *and* _____

_____.

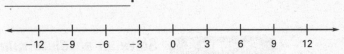

b. The distance between x and 0 is greater than $\frac{1}{4}$.

So, $x >$ ___ *or* $x <$ _____. The solutions are all real

numbers _____ *or* _____.

> Note that < can be replaced by ≤ and > can be replaced by ≥.

SOLVING ABSOLUTE VALUE INEQUALITIES

• The inequality $|ax + b| < c$ where $c > 0$ is equivalent to the compound inequality _____.

• The inequality $|ax + b| > c$ where $c > 0$ is equivalent to the compound inequality _____ *or* _____.

Example 2 *Solve an absolute value inequality*

Solve $|2x - 7| < 9$. Graph your solution.

Solution

$|2x - 7| < 9$ Write original inequality.

_____ $< 2x - 7 <$ _____   Rewrite as compound inequality.

_____   Add _____ to each expression.

_____   Divide each expression by _____.

The solutions are all real numbers _____
and _____. Check several solutions in the original
inequality.

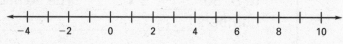

Example 3 *Solve an absolute value inequality*

Solve $|x + 8| - 4 \geq 2$. Graph your solution.

Solution

$|x + 8| - 4 \geq 2$ Write original
                                        inequality.

$|x + 8| \geq$ _____   Add _____ to
                                        each side.

$x + 8 \geq$ _____ *or* $x + 8 \leq$ _____   Rewrite as
                                        compound
                                        inequality.

$x \geq$ _____ *or* $x \leq$ _____   Subtract _____
                                        from each side.

The solutions are all real numbers _____
_____ *or* _____.

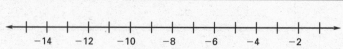

✔ *Checkpoint* **Solve the inequality. Graph your solution.**

1. $3|x - 6| > 9$

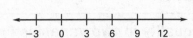

$-3 \quad 0 \quad 3 \quad 6 \quad 9 \quad 12$

2. $|6x - 11| \leq 7$

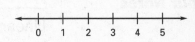

$0 \quad 1 \quad 2 \quad 3 \quad 4 \quad 5$

3. $-2|6x - 1| + 5 < 3$

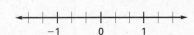

$-1 \qquad 0 \qquad 1$

SOLVING INEQUALITIES

One-Step and Multi-Step Inequalities

• Follow the steps for solving an equation, but _____ the inequality symbol when _____

_____.

Compound Inequalities

• If necessary, rewrite the inequality as two separate inequalities. Then solve each inequality separately. Include _____ or _____ in the solution.

Absolute Value Inequalities

• If necessary, isolate the absolute value expression on one side of the inequality. Rewrite the absolute value inequality as a _____. Then solve the compound inequality.

Homework

6.7 Graph Linear Inequalities in Two Variables

Goal • Graph linear inequalities in two variables.

Your Notes

VOCABULARY

Linear inequality in two variables

Graph of an inequality in two variables

Example 1   *Check solutions of a linear inequality*

Tell whether the ordered pair is a solution of $3x - 4y > 9$.

a. $(2, 0)$ b. $(2, -1)$

Solution

a. Test $(2, 0)$:

$3x - 4y > 9$ **Write inequality.**

$3(\underline{}) - 4(\underline{}) > 9$ **Substitute ___ for x and ___ for y.**

$\underline{} > 9$ **Simplify.**

$(2, 0)$ _____ a solution.

b. Test $(2, -1)$:

$3x - 4y > 9$ **Write inequality.**

$3(\underline{}) - 4(\underline{}) > 9$ **Substitute ___ for x and ____ for y.**

$\underline{} > 9$ **Simplify.**

$(2, -1)$ _____ a solution.

GRAPHING A LINEAR INEQUALITY IN TWO VARIABLES

Step 1 **Graph** the boundary line. Use a _____ line for < or >, and use a _____ line for ≤ or ≥.

Step 2 **Test** a point not on _____ by checking whether the ordered pair is a solution of the inequality.

Step 3 **Shade** the _____ containing the point if the ordered pair _____ a solution of the inequality. Shade the _____ if the ordered pair _____ a solution.

Example 2   *Graph a linear inequality in two variables*

Graph the inequality $y < -\frac{1}{2}x + 4$.

Solution

1. **Graph** the equation $y = -\frac{1}{2}x + 4$. The inequality is <, so use a _____ line.

2. **Test** (0, 0) in $y < -\frac{1}{2}x + 4$.

$$\underline{\quad} < -\frac{1}{2}(\underline{\quad}) + 4$$

$$\underline{\quad} < \underline{\quad}$$

3. _____ the half-plane that _____ (0, 0) because (0, 0) ____ a solution of the inequality.

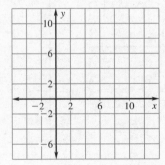

Example 3 *Graph a linear inequality in one variable*

Graph the inequality $x \geq 4$.

Solution

1. **Graph** the equation $x = 4$. The inequality is $\geq$, so use a _____ line.

2. **Test** $(0, 3)$ in $x \geq 4$. You only substitute the _____ because the inequality does not have the variable ___.

   ___ ≥ 4

3. _____ the half-plane that _____ $(0, 3)$, because $(0, 3)$ _____ a solution of the inequality.

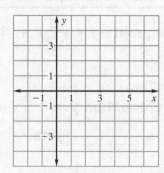

✔ *Checkpoint* **Graph the inequality.**

1. $2y + 4x > 8$

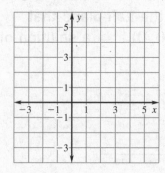

2. $y < 2$

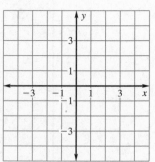

Homework

Words to Review

Give an example of the vocabulary word.

Graph of an inequality	Equivalent inequalities
Compound inequality	Absolute value equation
Absolute deviation	Linear inequality in two variables
Graph of a linear inequality in two variables	

Review your notes and Chapter 6 by using the Chapter Review on pages 415–418 of your textbook.

7.1 Solve Linear Systems by Graphing

Goal • Graph and solve systems of linear equations.

Your Notes

VOCABULARY

Systems of linear equations

Solution of a system of linear equations

Consistent independent system

SOLVING A LINEAR SYSTEM USING THE GRAPH-AND-CHECK METHOD

Step 1 _____ both equations in the same coordinate plane. For ease of graphing, you may want to write each equation in _____.

Step 2 Estimate the coordinates of the _____ _____.

Step 3 _____ the coordinates algebraically by substituting into each equation of the original linear system.

Example 1   *Use the graph-and-check method*

Solve the linear system: $3x + y = 9$ **Equation 1**

$x - y = 1$ **Equation 2**

Solution

1. _____ both equations.

> To ease graphing, write each equation in slope intercept form.

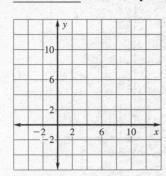

2. **Estimate** the point of intersection. The two lines appear to intersect at (___, ___).

3. **Check** whether (___, ___) is a solution by substituting ___ for x and ___ for y in each of the original equations.

Equation 1	Equation 2
$3x + y = 9$	$x - y = -1$
_____ $\overset{?}{=} 9$	_____ $\overset{?}{=} -1$
___ $= 9$ ✓	____ $= -1$ ✓

Because (___, ___) is a solution of each equation in the linear system, it is a _____.

✔ *Checkpoint* **Solve the linear system by graphing.**

1. $2y + 4x = 12$

$2x - y = -10$

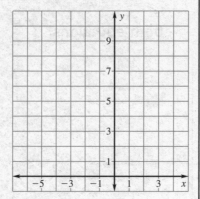

2. $4x + 2y = 6$

$3x - 3y = 9$

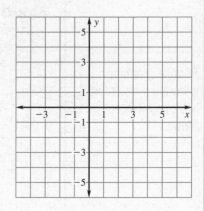

3. $2y = 6x + 8$

$4x + y = -3$

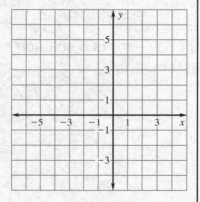

4. $y = 4x + 4$

$2y = -3x - 14$

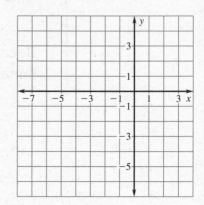

Homework

7.2 Solve Linear Systems by Substitution

Goal • Solve systems of linear equations by substitution.

Your Notes

SOLVING A LINEAR SYSTEM USING THE SUBSTITUTION METHOD

Step 1 _____ one of the equations for one of its variables. When possible, solve for a variable that has a coefficient of ___ or ____.

Step 2 _____ the expression from Step 1 into the other equation and solve for the other variable.

Step 3 _____ the value from Step 2 into the revised equation from Step 1 and solve.

Example 1   *Use the substitution method*

Solve the linear system: $x = -2y + 2$ **Equation 1**

$\qquad\qquad\qquad\qquad 3x + y = 16$ **Equation 2**

1. _____ for x. Equation 1 is already solved for x.

2. **Substitute** _____ for x in Equation 2 and solve for y.

$3x + y = 16$	Write Equation 2.
$3(\underline{\quad\quad}) + y = 16$	Substitute _____ for x.
$\underline{\quad\quad} + y = 16$	Distributive property
$\underline{\quad\quad} = 16$	Simplify.
$\underline{\quad} = \underline{\quad}$	Subtract ___ from each side.
$y = \underline{\quad}$	Divide each side by ____.

3. **Substitute** ____ for y in the original Equation 1 to find the value of x.

$x = -2y + 2 = -2(\underline{\quad}) + 2 = 4 + 2 = \underline{\quad}$

The solution is (___, _____).

> Remember to check your solution in each of the original equations.

Example 2   *Use the substitution method*

Solve the linear system: $4x - 2y = 14$ **Equation 1**

$2x + y = -3$ **Equation 2**

Solution

1. **Solve** Equation 2 for y.

$2x + y = -3$ **Write original Equation 2.**

$y = $ _____   **Revised Equation 2**

2. **Substitute** _____ for y in Equation 1 and solve for x.

$4x - 2y = 14$ **Write Equation 1.**

$4x - 2($_____$) = 14$ **Substitute** _____ **for y.**

$4x + $ _____ $= 14$ **Distributive property**

_____ $= 14$ **Simplify.**

____ $=$ ____   **Subtract** ____ **from each side.**

$x = $ ____   **Divide each side by** ____.

3. **Substitute** ____ for x in the revised Equation 2 to find the value of y.

$y = $ _____ $=$ _____ $=$ _____ $=$ ____

The solution is (____, ____).

✔ *Checkpoint* **Solve the linear system using the substitution method.**

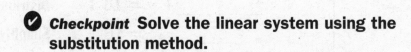

1. $5x - 4y = -1$	**2.** $x + y = 5$
$y = 6x + 5$	$7x - 9y = 3$

Homework

7.3 Solve Linear Systems by Adding or Subtracting

Goal • Solve linear systems using elimination.

SOLVING A LINEAR SYSTEM USING THE ELIMINATION METHOD

Step 1 _____ the equations to _____ one variable.

Step 2 _____ the resulting equation for the other variable.

Step 3 **Substitute** in either original equation to _____ _____ .

Example 1   *Use addition to eliminate a variable*

Solve the linear system: $x + 5y = 9$ **Equation 1**

$4x - 5y = -14$ **Equation 2**

Solution

1. _____ the equations to eliminate one variable.

$x + 5y = 9$
$4x - 5y = -14$
_____ = _____

2. **Solve for** x. $x =$ _____

3. **Substitute** _____ for x in either equation and _____ .

$x + 5y = 9$ **Write Equation 1.**

_____ $+ 5y = 9$ **Substitute** _____ for x.

$y =$ ___   **Solve for** y.

> Make sure to check your solution by substituting it into each of the original equations.

The solution is (_____, ___).

Example 2 *Use subtraction to eliminate a variable*

Solve the linear system: $3x - 4y = 2$ **Equation 1**

$3x + 2y = 26$ **Equation 2**

Solution

1. _____ the equations $3x - 4y = 2$

   to eliminate one variable. $\underline{3x + 2y = 26}$

                          $\underline{} = \underline{}$

2. **Solve** for y. $y = \underline{}$

3. **Substitute** ___ for y in either equation and

   _____.

   $3x + 2y = 26$ **Write Equation 2.**

   $3x + 2(\underline{}) = 26$ **Substitute** ___ **for** y.

   $x = \underline{}$ **Solve for** x.

The solution is (___ , ___).

✓ *Checkpoint* **Solve the linear system.**

1. $-8x + 3y = 12$	2. $x + 6y = 13$
$\ 8x - 9y = 12$	$\ -2x + 6y = -8$

Example 3 *Arrange like terms*

Solve the linear system: $6x + 7y = 16$ **Equation 1**

$y = 6x - 32$ **Equation 2**

Solution

1. _____ Equation 2 so that the like terms are arranged in columns.

$6x + 7y = 16$ → $6x + 7y = 16$

$y = 6x - 32$ _____

2. _____ the equations.   _____ = _____

3. **Solve** for y. $y =$ _____

4. **Substitute** _____ for y in either equation and _____ .

$6x + 7y = 16$ **Write Equation 1.**

$6x + 7(\_\_\_\_) = 16$ **Substitute** _____ for y.

$x =$ ___ _____ .

The solution is (___, _____).

✔ **Checkpoint** Solve the linear system.

3. $4x - 5y = 5$	4. $7y = 4 - 2x$
$5y = x + 10$	$2x + y = -8$

Homework

7.4 Solve Linear Systems by Multiplying First

Goal • Solve linear systems by multiplying first.

Your Notes

Example 1 *Multiply one equation, then add*

Solve the linear system: $3x - 3y = 21$ **Equation 1**

$8x + 6y = -14$ **Equation 2**

Solution

1. **Multiply** Equation 1 by ___ so that the coefficients of y are _____.

   $3x - 3y = 21$ $\times$ ___   _____

   $8x + 6y = -14$ $\underline{8x + 6y = -14}$

2. **Add** the equations.   _____ = ___

3. **Solve** for x. $x = $ ___

4. **Substitute** ___ for x in either of the original equations and _____.

   $3x - 3y = 21$ Write Equation 1.

   $3(\_\_\_) - 3y = 21$ Substitute ___ for x.

   $y = $ _____   Solve for y.

The solution is (_____, _____).

CHECK Substitute _____ for x and _____ for y in the original equations.

    Equation 1   Equation 2

    $3x - 3y = 21$ $8x + 6y = -14$

$3(\_\_\_) - 3(\_\_\_) \stackrel{?}{=} 21$ $8(\_\_\_) + 6(\_\_\_) \stackrel{?}{=} -14$

    _____ $= 21$ ✓   _____ $= -14$ ✓

Example 2 *Multiply both equations, then subtract*

Solve the linear system: $3y = -2x + 17$ **Equation 1**

                     $3x + 5y = 27$ **Equation 2**

Solution

1. **Arrange** the equations so that like terms are in columns.

   $2x + 3y = 17$ **Rewrite Equation 1.**

   $3x + 5y = 27$ **Write Equation 2.**

2. **Multiply** Equation 1 by ___ and Equation 2 by ___ so that the coefficient of x in each equation is the _____ _____ of 2 and 3, or ___.

   $2x + 3y = 17$ ×_ ⟶   ___x + ___y = ___

   $3x + 5y = 27$ ×_ ⟶   ___x + ___y = ___

3. _____ the equations.   _____ = ___

4. **Solve** for y. $y = $ ___

5. **Substitute** ___ for y in either of the original equations and solve for x.

   $3x + 5y = 27$ **Write Equation 2.**

   $3x + 5(\_\_) = 27$ **Substitute ___ for x.**

          $x = $ ___   **Solve for x.**

The solution is (___, ___).

✔ *Checkpoint* Solve the linear system using elimination.

1. $7x + 2y = 26$	**2.** $5y = 9x - 8$
$10x - 5y = -10$	$-20x + 10y = -10$

Homework

7.5 Solve Special Types of Linear Systems

Goal • Identify the number of solutions of a linear system.

Your Notes

VOCABULARY

Inconsistent system

Consistent dependent system

Example 1   A linear system with no solutions

Show that the linear system has no solution.

$-2x + y = 1$ **Equation 1**

$-2x + y = -3$ **Equation 2**

Solution

> To ease graphing, write each equation in slope intercept form.

Method 1 Graphing

Graph the linear system.

The lines are _____ because they have the same slope but different y-intercepts. Parallel lines do _____, so the system has _____.

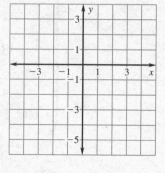

Method 2 Elimination

Subtract the equations.

$$-2x + y = 1$$
$$\underline{-2x + y = -3}$$
$$\underline{\quad} = \underline{\quad}$$

The variables are _____ and you are left with a _____ regardless of the values of x and y. This tells you that the system has _____.

Example 2 *A linear system with infinitely many solutions*

Show that the linear system has infinitely many solutions.

$x + 3y = -3$ **Equation 1**

$3x + 9y = -9$ **Equation 2**

Solution

Method 1 Graphing

Graph the linear system.
The equations represent the
_____, so any point
on the line is a solution.
So, the linear system has

_____.

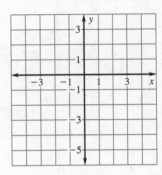

Method 2 Substitution

$x =$ _____   **Solve Equation 1 for x.**

$3x + 9y = -9$ **Write Equation 2.**

$3($ _____ $) + 9y = -9$ **Substitute _____ for x.**

_____ $+ 9y = -9$ **Distributive property**

_____ $= -9$ **Simplify.**

The variables are _____ and you are left with a
statement that is _____ regardless of the values of
x and y. This tells you that the system has _____

_____.

✔ *Checkpoint* **Tell whether the linear system has no solution or infinitely many solutions.**

1. $y = 2x - 7$	**2.** $2y = 8x + 4$
$4x - 2y = 14$	$-4x + y = 4$

NUMBER OF SOLUTIONS OF A LINEAR SYSTEM

One solution	No solution	Infinitely many solutions
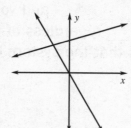	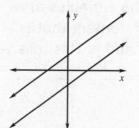	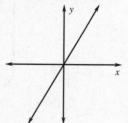

The lines
_____.
The lines have
_____
slopes.

The lines
are _____.
The lines
have the
same slope
and _____
y-intercepts.

The lines
_____.
The lines have
the same slope
and the _____
_____.

7.6 Solve Linear Systems of Linear Inequalities

Goal • Solve systems of linear inequalities in two variables.

Your Notes

VOCABULARY

System of linear inequalities
_____

Solution of a system of linear inequalities
_____

Graph of a system of linear inequalities

GRAPHING A SYSTEM OF LINEAR INEQUALITIES

Step 1 _____ each inequality.

Step 2 **Find** the _____ of the graphs. The graph of the system is this intersection.

Example 1   *Graph a system of three linear inequalities*

Graph the system of inequalities.

$y > 1$	**Inequality 1**
$x \leq 4$	**Inequality 2**
$3y < 6x - 6$	**Inequality 3**

Solution

Graph all three inequalities in the same coordinate plane. The graph of the system is the _____ shown.

The region is _____ the line $y = 1$.

The region is _____ _____ of the line $x = 4$.

The region is _____ the line $3y = 6x - 6$.

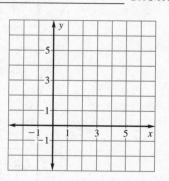

✓ *Checkpoint* **Graph the system of linear equations.**

1. $x + y \leq 5$

    $y < x + 3$

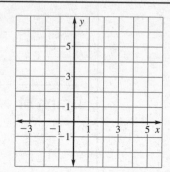

---

2. $x > -2$

    $y \leq 4$

    $3x + 4y \leq 24$

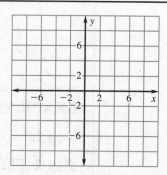

Example 2 | *Write a system of linear inequalities*

Write a system of inequalities for the shaded region.

Solution

Inequality 1 One boundary line for the shaded region is _____. Because the shaded region is _____ the _____ line, the inequality is _____.

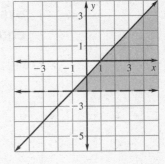

Inequality 2 Another boundary line for the shaded region has a slope of ___ and a *y*-intercept of _____. So, its equation is _____. Because the shaded region is _____ the _____ line, the inequality is _____.

The system of inequalities for the shaded region is:

_____   **Inequality 1**

_____   **Inequality 2**

✔ *Checkpoint* Write a system of inequalities that defines the shaded region.

3.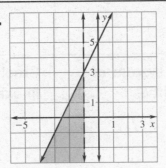

4.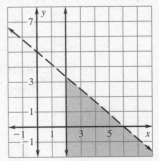

Homework

Words to Review

Give an example of the vocabulary word.

System of linear equations	Solution of a system of linear equations
Consistent independent system	Inconsistent system
Dependent system	System of linear inequalities
Solution of a system of linear inequalities	Graph of a system of linear inequalities

Review your notes and Chapter 7 by using the Chapter Review on pages 475–478 of your textbook.

8.1 Apply Exponent Properties Involving Products

Goal • Use properties of exponents involving products.

Your Notes

VOCABULARY

Order of magnitude

PRODUCT OF POWERS PROPERTY

Let a be a real number, and let m and n be positive integers.

Words: To multiply powers having the same base, _____

_____.

Algebra: $a^m \cdot a^n = a$_____

Example: $5^6 \cdot 5^3 = 5$_____ $= 5$___

Example 1 *Use the product of powers property*

Simplify the expression.

a. $2^2 \cdot 2^3 = 2$_____

  $= 2$___

b. $w^9 \cdot w^2 \cdot w^7 = w$_____

   $= w$___

> When simplifying powers with numerical bases only, write your answers using exponents.

c. $4^4 \cdot 4 = 4^4 \cdot 4$___

  $= 4$_____

  $= 4$___

d. $(-6)(-6)^6 = (-6)$___ $\cdot (-6)^6$

   $= (-6)$_____

   $= (-6)$___

POWER OF A POWER PROPERTY

Let a be a real number, and let m and n be positive integers.

Words: To find a power of a power, _____.

Algebra: $(a^m)^n = a$____

Example: $(3^4)^2 = 3$____ $= 3$__

Example 2   *Use the power of a power property*

Simplify the expression.

a. $(5^2)^3 = 5$____ $= 5$__

b. $(n^7)^2 = n$____ $= n$__

c. $[(-3)^5]^3 = (-3)$____

            $= (-3)$__

d. $[(z-4)^2]^5 = (z-4)$____

               $= (z-4)$__

POWER OF A PRODUCT PROPERTY

Let a and b be real numbers, and let m be a positive integer.

Words: To find a power of a product, find the _____

_____.

Algebra: $(ab)^m =$ _____

Example: $(23 \cdot 17)^5 =$ _____

Example 3   *Use the power of a product property*

Simplify the expression.

a. $(4 \cdot 16)^7 =$ _____

b. $(-3rs)^2 = ($_____$)^2 = ($____$)^2 \cdot$ __$^2 \cdot$ __^{2}

                $=$ _____

c. $-(3rs)^2 = -($_____$)^2 = -($__$^2 \cdot$ __$^2 \cdot$ __$^2)$

                $=$ _____

> When simplifying powers with numerical and variable bases, evaluate the numerical power.

✓ *Checkpoint* **Simplify the expression.**

1. $(-7)^8(-7)^5$	**2.** $k^3 \cdot k \cdot k^2$	**3.** $(p^3)^4$
4. $[(q + 8)^2]^6$	**5.** $(8cd)^2$	**6.** $-(5z)^3$

Example 4   *Use all three properties*

Simplify $x^2 \cdot (3x^3y)^3$**.**

Solution

$x^2 \cdot (3x^3y)^3 =$ _____   _____

_____ property

$=$ _____

_____ property

$=$ _____

_____ property

✓ *Checkpoint* **Simplify the expression.**

7. $(2x^5)^4$	**8.** $(3y^3)^4 \cdot y^5$

8.2 Apply Exponent Properties Involving Quotients

Goal • Use properties of exponents involving quotients.

> **QUOTIENT OF POWERS PROPERTY**
>
> Let a be a nonzero real number, and let m and n be positive integers such that $m > n$.
>
> **Words:** To divide powers having the same base, _____ the exponents.
>
> **Algebra:** $\dfrac{a^m}{a^n} = a$ _____ , $a \neq 0$
>
> **Example:** $\dfrac{4^7}{4^2} = 4$ _____ $= 4$ ___

Example 1   *Use the quotient of powers property*

Simplify the expression.

a. $\dfrac{6^{12}}{6^5} = 6$ _____ $= 6$ ___

b. $\dfrac{(-2)^7}{(-2)^4} = (-2)$ _____ $= (-2)$ ___

c. $\dfrac{4^2 \cdot 4^8}{4^4} = \dfrac{4 \underline{\quad}}{4^4}$

      $= 4$ _____

      $=$ ___

> When simplifying powers with numerical bases only, write your answers using exponents.

d. $\dfrac{1}{y^9} \cdot y^{12} = \dfrac{y^{12}}{y^9}$

      $= y$ _____

      $=$ ___

POWER OF A QUOTIENT PROPERTY

Let a and b be real numbers with $b \neq 0$, and let m be a positive integer.

Words: To find a power of a quotient, find the power of the _____ and the power of the _____ and divide.

Algebra: $\left(\dfrac{a}{b}\right)^m =$ ____ , $b \neq 0$ **Example:** $\left(\dfrac{4}{7}\right)^3 =$ ____

Example 2   *Use the power of a quotient property*

Simplify the expression.

> When simplifying powers with numerical and variable bases, evaluate the numerical power.

a. $\left(\dfrac{r}{s}\right)^5 =$ ____

b. $\left(-\dfrac{4}{w}\right)^3 = \left(\right)^3 =$ ____ ____ = ____ = ____

✔ *Checkpoint* **Simplify the expression.**

1. $\dfrac{(-8)^8}{(-8)^5}$	**2.** $\dfrac{3^5 \cdot 3^4}{3^3}$
3. $\left(-\dfrac{r}{3}\right)^2$	**4.** $\left(\dfrac{5}{t}\right)^4$

Example 3   *Use properties of exponents*

Simplify $\left(\dfrac{2y^7}{y^5}\right)^3$.

Solution

$\left(\dfrac{2y^7}{y^5}\right)^3 = \dfrac{\underline{\hphantom{xxx}}}{\underline{\hphantom{xxx}}}$ _____ **property**

$\hphantom{\left(\dfrac{2y^7}{y^5}\right)^3} = \dfrac{\underline{\hphantom{xxx}}}{\underline{\hphantom{xxx}}}$ _____ **property**

$\hphantom{\left(\dfrac{2y^7}{y^5}\right)^3} = \dfrac{\underline{\hphantom{xxx}}}{\underline{\hphantom{xxx}}}$ _____ **property**

$\hphantom{\left(\dfrac{2y^7}{y^5}\right)^3} = \underline{\hphantom{xxx}}$ _____ **property**

✔ *Checkpoint* **Simplify the expression.**

5. $\left(\dfrac{7y^3z}{y}\right)^2$	**6.** $\dfrac{2s^4}{t} \cdot \left(\dfrac{2t}{s}\right)^3$
7. $\left(\dfrac{6m^3n^2}{3mn}\right)^3$	**8.** $\dfrac{4a}{b^2} \cdot \left(\dfrac{2a^2b^3}{a}\right)^4$

Homework

Define and Use Zero and Negative Exponents

Goal • Use zero and negative exponents.

DEFINITION OF ZERO AND NEGATIVE EXPONENTS		
Words	**Algebra**	**Example**
a to the zero power is 1.	$a^0 = \underline{\quad}, a \neq 0$	$5^0 = \underline{\quad}$
a^{-n} is the reciprocal of a^n.	$a^{-n} = \dfrac{\quad}{\quad}, a \neq 0$	$2^{-1} = \dfrac{\quad}{\quad}$
a^n is the reciprocal of a^{-n}.	$a^n = \dfrac{\quad}{\quad}, a \neq 0$	$2 = \dfrac{\quad}{\quad}$

Example 1 *Use definition of zero and negative exponents*

Evaluate the expression.

a. $2^{-3} = \dfrac{\quad}{\quad}$ Definition of _____
                                         _____

$= \dfrac{\quad}{\quad}$ Evaluate exponent.

b. $(-10)^0 = \underline{\quad}$ Definition of _____

c. $\left(\dfrac{1}{4}\right)^{-3} = \dfrac{\quad}{\quad}$ Definition of _____
                                                                  _____

$=$ __   Evaluate exponent.

$= \underline{\quad}$ Simplify.

d. $0^{-7} = \underline{\qquad\qquad}$ a^{-n} is defined only for
                                              a _____ number a.

PROPERTIES OF EXPONENTS

Let *a* and *b* be real numbers, and let *m* and *n* be integers.

$a^m \cdot a^n = a$_____ _____ property

$(a^m)^n = a$____ _____ property

$(ab)^m =$ _____ _____ property

$\dfrac{a^m}{a^n} = a$_____ $, a \neq 0$ _____ property

$\left(\dfrac{a}{b}\right)^m =$ ____ $, b \neq 0$ _____ property

---

Example 2   *Evaluate exponential expressions*

Evaluate the expression.

a. $(-5)^4 \cdot (-5)^{-4} =$ _____   **Product of powers property**

$=$ _____   _____ **exponents.**

$=$ ___   **Definition of** _____

b. $(5^{-2})^{-2} =$ _____   _____ _____ **property**

$=$ ____   _____ **exponents.**

$=$ ____   **Evaluate power.**

c. $\dfrac{1}{4^{-2}} =$ ____   **Definition of** _____ _____

$=$ ____   **Evaluate power.**

d. $\dfrac{3^2}{3^{-1}} =$ _____   _____ _____ **property**

$=$ ____   _____ **exponents.**

$=$ ____   **Evaluate power.**

✔ Checkpoint Evaluate the expression.

1. $\left(\frac{1}{8}\right)^{-1}$	2. $\frac{1}{3^{-2}}$
3. $\frac{6^{-1}}{6}$	4. $(5^{-1})^2$

Example 3 — Use properties of exponents

Simplify the expression $\dfrac{2w^{-3}x}{(2wx)^2}$. Write your answer using only positive exponents.

Solution

$\dfrac{2w^{-3}x}{(2wx)^2} = $ _____ **Definition of negative exponents**

$= $ _____ _____ **property**

$= $ _____ _____ **property**

$= $ _____ _____ **property**

✔ Checkpoint Simplify the expression.

5. $\dfrac{6fg^{-4}}{2f^2g}$	6. $(3yz^2)^{-2}$

Homework

8.4 Use Scientific Notation

Goal • Read and write numbers in scientific notation.

VOCABULARY

Scientific notation

SCIENTIFIC NOTATION

A number is written in scientific notation when it is of the form _____ where $1 \le c < 10$ and n is an integer.

Number	Standard form	Scientific notation
Sixteen million	_____	_____
Two hundredths	_____	_____

Example 1 *Write numbers in scientific notation*

a. $7,820,000 =$ _____ $\times 10$___

Move decimal point ___ places to the _____. Exponent is _____.

b. $0.00401 =$ _____ $\times 10$___

Move decimal point ___ places to the _____. Exponent is _____.

Example 2 *Write numbers in standard form*

a. $3.89 \times 10^9 =$ _____

Exponent is _____. Move decimal point ___ places to the _____.

b. $9.097 \times 10^{-5} =$ _____

Exponent is _____. Move decimal point ___ places to the _____.

Your Notes

✓ **Checkpoint Complete the following exercise.**

> **1.** Write the number 0.0899 in scientific notation. Then write the number 6.0001×10^7 in standard form.

Example 3 Order numbers in scientific notation

Order 3.2×10^{-4}, 0.0004, and 2.8×10^{-5} from least to greatest.

Solution

Step 1 Write each number in scientific notation, if necessary.

$0.0004 = $ _____

Step 2 Order the numbers. First order the numbers with different powers of 10. Then order the numbers with the same power of 10.

Because 10^{-5} ___ 10^{-4}, you know that _____ is less than both _____ and _____. Because 3.2 ___ 4, you know that _____ is less than _____.

So, _____ < _____ < _____.

Step 3 Write the original numbers in order from least to greatest.

_____

✓ **Checkpoint Complete the following exercise.**

> **2.** Order 225,000, 1,740,000, and 1.75×10^5 from least to greatest.

Example 4	*Compute with numbers in scientific notation*

Evaluate the expression. Write your answer in scientific notation.

a. $(5.6 \times 10^{-4})(1.4 \times 10^{-5})$

$= (5.6 \cdot 1.4) \times (10^{-4} \cdot 10^{-5})$ Commutative property and associative property

$= \underline{\hspace{2cm}} \times \underline{\hspace{2cm}}$ Product of powers property

b. $(3.2 \times 10^2)^3$

$= \underline{\hspace{2cm}} \times \underline{\hspace{2cm}}$ Power of a product property

$= \underline{\hspace{2cm}} \times \underline{\hspace{2cm}}$ Power of a power property

$= (\underline{\hspace{3cm}}) \times \underline{\hspace{2cm}}$ Write $\underline{\hspace{2cm}}$ in scientific notation.

$= \underline{\hspace{2cm}} \times (\underline{\hspace{2cm}})$ Associative property

$= \underline{\hspace{3cm}}$ Product of powers property

c. $\dfrac{3.5 \times 10^{-3}}{1.75 \times 10^{-5}}$

$= \dfrac{3.5}{1.75} \times \dfrac{10^{-3}}{10^{-5}}$ Product rule for fractions

$= \underline{\hspace{1.5cm}} \times \underline{\hspace{1.5cm}}$ Quotient of powers property

---

✔ **Checkpoint** **Simplify the expression.**

3. $(2.01 \times 10^{-7})^2$

4. $\dfrac{4.8 \times 10^{-4}}{6 \times 10^{-4}}$

Homework

8.5 Write and Graph Exponential Growth Functions

Goal • Write and graph exponential growth models.

Your Notes

VOCABULARY

Exponential function

Exponential growth

Compound interest

Example 1   *Write a function rule*

Write a rule for the function.

x	-2	-1	0	1	2
y	$\frac{2}{9}$	$\frac{2}{3}$	2	6	8

Solution

Step 1 **Tell** whether the function is exponential. Here the y-values are multiplied by ____ for each increase of 1 in x, so the table represents an exponential function of the form _____ where _____.

Step 2 **Find** the value of a by finding the value of y when $x = 0$. When $x = 0$, $y =$ _____ $=$ _____ $=$ ____. The value of y when $x = 0$ is ____, so _____.

Step 3 **Write** the function rule. A rule for the function is $y =$ _____.

Example 2 *Graph an exponential function*

Graph the function $y = 3^x$. Identify its domain and range.

Solution

Step 1 Make a table by choosing a few values for *x* and finding the values of *y*. The domain is _____.

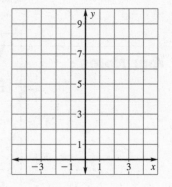

x	−2	−1	0	1	2
y	___	___	___	___	___

Step 2 Plot the points.

Step 3 Draw a smooth curve through the points. From either the table or the graph, you can see that the range is _____.

Example 3 *Compare graphs of exponential functions*

Graph $y = 2 \cdot 3^x$. Compare the graph with the graph of $y = 3^x$.

Solution

To graph each function, make a table of values, plot the points, and draw a smooth curve through the points.

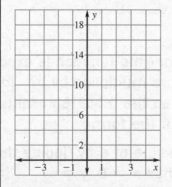

x	$y = 3^x$	$y = 2 \cdot 3^x$
−2	___	___
−1	___	___
0	___	___
1	___	___
2	___	___

Because the *y*-values for $y = 2 \cdot 3^x$ are _____ the corresponding *y*-values for $y = 3^x$, the graph of $y = 2 \cdot 3^x$ is a _____ of the graph of $y = 3^x$.

✅ *Checkpoint* **Complete the following exercises.**

1. Write a rule for the function.

x	−2	−1	0	1	2
y	$-\frac{1}{16}$	$-\frac{1}{4}$	−1	−4	−16

2. Graph $y = 4^x$. Identify its domain and range.

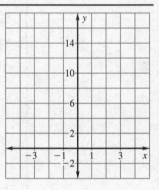

3. Graph $y = -2 \cdot 3^x$. Compare the graph with the graph of $y = 3^x$.

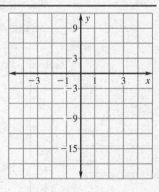

EXPONENTIAL GROWTH MODEL

$y = a(1 + r)^t$

a is the _____. r is the _____.

$1 + r$ is the _____. t is the _____.

Example 4 *Solve a compound interest problem*

Investment You put $250 in a savings account that earns 4% annual interest compounded yearly. You do not make any deposits or withdrawals. How much will your investment be worth in 10 years?

Solution

The initial amount is _____, the interest rate is _____, or _____, and the time period is _____.

$y = a(1 + r)t$ Write exponential growth model.

$= $ _____$(1 + $ _____$)$——   Substitute _____ for a, _____ for r, and ____ for t.

$= 250($_____$)^{10}$ Simplify.

$\approx$ _____   Use a calculator.

You will have _____ in 10 years.

✔ *Checkpoint* **Complete the following exercise.**

4. In Example 4, suppose the annual interest rate is 5%. How much will your investment be worth in 10 years?

Homework

8.6 Write and Graph Exponential Decay Functions

Goal • Write and graph exponential decay functions.

VOCABULARY

Exponential decay

Example 1   *Graph an exponential function*

Graph the function $y = \left(\frac{1}{3}\right)^x$ and identify its domain and range.

Solution

Step 1 Make a table of values.
The domain is _____ _____.

x	−2	−1	0	1	2
y	__	__	__	__	__

Step 2 Plot the points.

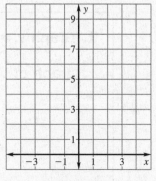

Step 3 Draw a smooth curve through the points. From either the table or the graph, you can see that the range is _____.

Example 2   *Compare graphs of exponential functions*

Graph $y = 2 \cdot \left(\frac{1}{3}\right)^x$. Compare the graph with the graph

of $y = \left(\frac{1}{3}\right)^x$.

Solution

x	$y = \left(\frac{1}{3}\right)^x$	$y = 2 \cdot \left(\frac{1}{3}\right)^x$
-2	___	___
-1	___	___
0	___	___
1	___	___
2	___	___

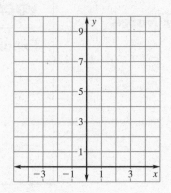

Because the y-values for $y = 2 \cdot \left(\frac{1}{3}\right)^x$ are _____

the corresponding y-values for $y = \left(\frac{1}{3}\right)^x$, the graph of

$y = 2 \cdot \left(\frac{1}{3}\right)^x$ is a _____ of the graph of

$y = \left(\frac{1}{3}\right)^x$.

✔ *Checkpoint* **Complete the following exercise.**

1. Graph $y = -2 \cdot \left(\frac{1}{3}\right)^x$. Compare the graph with the

graph of $\left(\frac{1}{3}\right)^x$.

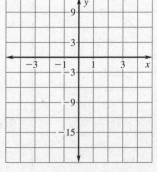

Example 3 *Classify and write rules for functions*

Tell whether the graph represents *exponential growth* or *exponential decay*. Then write a rule for the function.

Solution

The graph represents

_____

($y = ab^x$ where $0 < b < 1$).
The y-intercept is ____, so
$a =$ ____. Find the value
of b by using the point
(1, 1) and $a =$ ____.

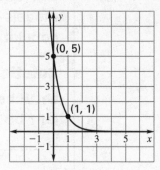

$y = ab^x$ Write function.

___ $=$ ___ $\cdot b$—   Substitute.

_____ $= b$ Solve.

A function rule is _____.

EXPONENTIAL GROWTH AND DECAY

Exponential Growth

$y = ab^x, a > 0$
and $b > 1$

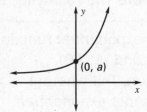

Exponential Decay

$y = ab^x, a > 0$
and $0 < b < 1$

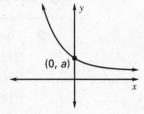

EXPONENTIAL DECAY MODEL

$y = a(1 + r)^t$

a is the _____. r is the _____.

$1 - r$ is the _____. t is the _____.

Example 4   Use the exponential decay model

Population The population of a city decreased from 1995 to 2003 by 1.5% annually. In 1995 there were about 357,000 people living in the city. Write a function that models the city's population since 1995. Then find the population in 2003.

Solution

Let P be the population of the city (in thousands), and let t be the time (in years) since 1995. The initial value is _____, and the decay rate is _____.

$P = a(1 - r)^t$ Write exponential decay model.

$= \underline{\hspace{1cm}}(1 - \underline{\hspace{1.5cm}})^t$ Substitute _____ for a, and _____ for r.

$= \underline{\hspace{2cm}}$ Simplify.

To find the population in 2003, ___ years after 1995, substitute ___ for t.

$P = \underline{\hspace{3cm}}$ Substitute ___ for t.

$\approx \underline{\hspace{1.5cm}}$ Use a calculator.

The city's population was about _____ in 2003.

✔ *Checkpoint* **Complete the following exercises.**

2. The graph of an exponential function passes through the points (0, 4) and (1, 10). Graph the function. Tell whether the graph represents *exponential growth* or *exponential decay*. Then write a rule for the function.

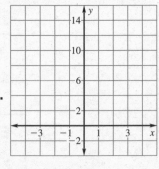

Homework

3. In Example 4, suppose that the decay rate of the city's population remains the same beyond 2003. What will be the population in 2020?

Words to Review

Give an example of the vocabulary word.

Order of magnitude	Scientific notation
Exponential function	Exponential growth
Compound interest	Exponential decay

Review your notes and Chapter 8 by using the Chapter Review on pages 543–546 of your textbook.

9.1 Add and Subtract Polynomials

Goal • Add and subtract polynomials.

Your Notes

VOCABULARY

Monomial

Degree of a monomial

Polynomial

Degree of a polynomial

Leading coefficient

Binomial

Trinomial

Example 1   *Rewrite a polynomial*

Write $7 + 2x^4 - 4x$ so that the exponents decrease from left to right. Identify the degree and leading coefficient of the polynomial.

Solution

Consider the degree of each of the polynomial's terms.

Degree is ___.   Degree is ___.   Degree is ___.

$$7 + 2x^4 - 4x$$

The polynomial can be written as _____. The greatest degree is ___, so the degree of the polynomial is ___, and the leading coefficient is ___.

Your Notes

✓ *Checkpoint* **Write the polynomial so that the exponents decrease from left to right. Identify the degree and leading coefficient of the polynomial.**

---

1. $5x + 13 + 8x^3$

---

2. $4y^4 - 7y^5 + 2y$

Example 2   *Identify and classify polynomials*

Tell whether the expression is a polynomial. If it is a polynomial, find its degree and classify it by the number of terms. Otherwise, tell why it is not a polynomial.

	Expression	Is it a polynomial?	Classify by degree and number of terms
a.	-6	_____	0 degree monomial
b.	$m^{-3} + 4$	_____ _____	
c.	$-h^3 + 4h^2$	Yes	_____ _____
d.	$9 - 5x^4 + 3x$	Yes	_____ _____
e.	$2w^3 + 4^w$	_____ _____	

✓ *Checkpoint* **Tell whether the expression is a polynomial. If it is a polynomial, find its degree and classify it by the number of terms. Otherwise, tell why it is not a polynomial.**

---

3. $4x - x^7 + 5x^3$	**4.** $v^3 + v^{-2} + 2v$

Example 3 Add polynomials

Find the sum (a) $(4x^3 + x^2 - 5) + (7x + x^3 - 3x^2)$ and (b) $(x^2 + x + 8) + (x^2 - x - 1)$.

Solution

a. **Vertical format:** Align like terms in vertical columns.

$$4x^3 + \ x^2 \qquad\quad - 5$$
$$+ \ \ x^3 - 3x^2 + 7x$$
_____

If a particular power of the variable appears in one polynomial but not the other, leave a space in that column, or write the term with a coefficient of 0.

b. **Horizontal format:** Group like terms and simplify.

$(x^2 + x + 8) + (x^2 - x - 1)$

$= ($ _____ $) + ($ _____ $) + ($ _____ $)$

$=$ _____

Example 4 Subtract polynomials

Find the difference (a) $(4z^2 - 3) - (-2z^2 + 5z - 1)$ and (b) $(3x^2 + 6x - 4) - (x^2 - x - 7)$.

Solution

a.
$$(\ \ 4z^2 \qquad\quad - 3)$$
$$- (-2z^2 + 5z - 1)$$
_____

$$4z^2 \qquad\qquad - 3$$
$$\underline{}2z^2 \ \underline{} \ 5z \ \underline{} \ 1$$
_____

Remember to multiply *each* term in the polynomial by -1 when you write the subtraction as addition.

b. $(3x^2 + 6x - 4) - (x^2 - x - 7)$

$= 3x^2 + 6x - 4$ _____

$=$ _____

$=$ _____

✓ *Checkpoint* **Find the sum or difference.**

Homework

5. $(3x^4 - 2x^2 - 1) + (5x^3 - x^2 + 9x^4)$

_____

6. $(3t^2 - 5t + t^4) - (11t^4 - 3t^2)$

9.2 Multiply Polynomials

Goal • Multiply polynomials.

Your Notes

Example 1 *Multiply a monomial and a polynomial*

Find the product $3x^3(2x^3 - x^2 - 7x - 3)$.

Solution

$3x^3(2x^3 - x^2 - 7x - 3)$

$= 3x^3(\underline{\quad}) - 3x^3(\underline{\quad}) - 3x^3(\underline{\quad}) - 3x^3(\underline{\quad})$

$= \underline{\quad} - \underline{\quad} - \underline{\quad} - \underline{\quad}$

Example 2 *Multiply polynomials vertically and horizontally*

Find the product.

a. $(a^2 - 6a - 3)(2a - 5)$ **b.** $(3b^2 - 2b + 5)(5b - 6)$

Solution

> Remember that the terms of $(2a - 5)$ are $2a$ and -5. They are *not* $2a$ and 5.

a. Vertical format:

$$
\begin{array}{r}
a^2 - \quad 6a - 3 \\
\times \qquad\quad 2a - 5 \\
\hline
-\underline{\quad}a^2 + \underline{\quad}a + \underline{\quad} \\
\underline{\quad}a^3 - \underline{\quad}a^2 - \underline{\quad}a \\
\hline
\end{array}
$$

Write the product in vertical format.

Multiply by _____.

Multiply by _____.

Add products.

b. Horizontal format:

$(3b^2 - 2b + 5)(5b - 6)$

$= \underline{\quad}(5b - 6) - \underline{\quad}(5b - 6)$
$\quad + \underline{\quad}(5b - 6)$

$= \underline{\hspace{4cm}}$

$= \underline{\hspace{4cm}}$

Copyright © McDougal Littell/Houghton Mifflin Company.

Lesson 9.2 • **Algebra 1 Notetaking Guide**   191

✅ *Checkpoint* **Find the product.**

1. $2x^2(x^3 - 5x^2 + 3x - 7)$

2. $(a^2 + 5a - 4)(2a + 3)$

Example 3   *Multiply binomials using the FOIL pattern*

Find the product $(2c + 7)(c - 9)$**.**

Solution

$(2c + 7)(c - 9)$

     $= 2c(\underline{}) + 2c(\underline{}) + 7(\underline{}) + 7(\underline{})$

     $= \underline{}$

     $= \underline{}$

✅ *Checkpoint* **Complete the following exercise.**

3. Find the product $(m + 3)(5m - 4)$**.**

Example 4   *Multiply ponynomials to find an area*

Area The dimensions of a rectangle are $x + 4$ and $x + 5$. Write an expression that represents the area of the rectangle.

Solution

Area = length · width   Formula for area of a rectangle

= (_____)(_____)   Substitute for length and width.

= _____   Multiply binomials.

= _____   Combine like terms.

CHECK   Use a graphing calculator to check your answer. Graph
y_1 = _____ and
y_2 = _____ in the same viewing window. The graphs _____, so the product of $x + 4$ and $x + 5$ is _____.

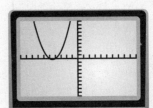

✔ *Checkpoint* **Complete the following exercise.**

4. The dimensions of a rectangle are $x + 3$ and $x + 11$. Write an expression that represents the area of the rectangle.

Example 5   *Solve a multi-step problem*

Walkway You are making a a walkway around part of your swimming pool. The dimensions of the swimming pool and walkway are shown in the diagram.

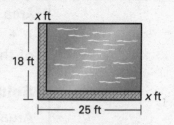

x ft

18 ft

x ft

25 ft

- Write a polynomial that represents the area of the swimming pool.

- What is the area of the swimming pool if the walkway is 2 feet wide?

Solution

Step 1 Write a polynomial using the formula for the area of a rectangle. The length is _____. The width is _____.

Area = _____ • _____

= _____

= _____

= _____

Step 2 Substitute ____ for *x* and evaluate.

Area = _____ = _____

The area of the swimming pool is _____.

✔ *Checkpoint* **Complete the following exercise.**

5. Swimming Pool Your neighbor has a walkway around his entire pool as shown in the diagram. The width of the walkway is the same on every side. Write a polynomial that represents the area of the pool. What is the area of the pool if the walkway is 3 feet wide?

x ft

22 ft

30 ft

x ft

Homework

9.3 Find Special Products of Polynomials

Goal • Use special product patterns to multiply polynomials.

Your Notes

SQUARE OF A BINOMIAL PATTERN

Algebra

$(a + b)^2 = a^2$ _____ $+ b^2$

$(a - b)^2 = a^2$ _____ $+ b^2$

Example

$(x + 4)^2 = x^2$ _____ $+ 16$

$(3x - 2)^2 = 9x^2$ _____ $+ 4$

Example 1   *Use the square of a binomial pattern*

Find the product.

Solution

> When you use special product patterns, remember that *a* and *b* can be numbers, variables, or variable expressions.

a. $(4x + 3)^2 = (4x)^2$ _____ $+ 3^2$

$= 16x^2$ _____ $+ 9$

b. $(3x - 5y)^2 = (3x)^2$ _____ $+ (5y)^2$

$= 9x^2$ _____ $+ 25y^2$

✔ **Checkpoint** **Find the product.**

1. $(x + 9)^2$

2. $(2x - 7)^2$

3. $(5r + s)^2$

SUM AND DIFFERENCE PATTERN

Algebra

$(a + b)(a - b) =$ ___^{2} − ___^{2}

Example

$(x + 4)(x - 4) =$ ___^{2} − ___

Example 2 *Use the sum and difference pattern*

Find the product.

Solution

a. $(n + 3)(n - 3) =$ ___^{2} − ___^{2} Sum and difference pattern

$=$ ___^{2} − ___   Simplify.

b. $(4x + y)(4x - y) =$ ___^{2} − ___^{2} Sum and difference pattern

$=$ ___^{2} − ___^{2} Simplify.

Example 3 *Use special products and mental math*

Use special products to find the product 17 · 23.

Solution

Notice that 17 is 3 less than ___ while 23 is 3 more than ___.

$17 \cdot 23 = ($ ___ $- 3)($ ___ $+ 3)$ Write as product.

$=$ _____   Sum and difference pattern

$=$ _____   Evaluate powers.

$=$ ___   Simplify.

✓ *Checkpoint* **Complete the following exercises.**

4. Find the product $(z + 6)(z - 6)$.

5. Find the product $(4x + 3)(4x - 3)$.

6. Find the product $(x + 5y)(x - 5y)$.

7. *Describe* how you can use special products to find 39^2.

Example 4   *Solve a multi-step problem*

Eye Color An offspring's eye color is determined by a combination of two genes, one inherited from each parent. Each parent has two color genes, and the offspring has an equal chance of inheriting either one.

The gene *B* is for brown eyes, and the gene *b* is for blue eyes. Any gene combination with a *B* results in brown eyes. Suppose each parent has the same gene combination *Bb*. The Punnett square shows the possible gene

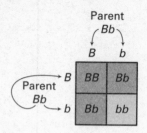

combinations of the offspring and the resulting eye color.

• What percent of the possible gene combinations of the offspring result in blue eyes?

• Show how you could use a polynomial to model the possible gene combinations of the offspring.

Solution

Step 1 **Notice** that the Punnett square shows that ____ out of 4, or _____ of the possible gene combinations result in blue eyes.

Step 2 **Model** the gene from each parent with _____. The possible gene of the offspring can be modeled by _____. Notice that this product also represents the area of the Punnett square.

_____

= _____

= _____

The coefficients show that _____ of the possible gene combinations will result in blue eyes.

✔ *Checkpoint* **Complete the following exercise.**

8. **Eye Color** Look back at Example 4. What percent of the possible gene combinations of the offspring result in brown eyes?

9.4 Solve Polynomial Equations in Factored Form

Goal • Solve polynomial equations.

Your Notes

VOCABULARY

Roots

Vertical motion model

ZERO-PRODUCT PROPERTY

Let a and b be real numbers. If $ab = 0$, then ___ = 0 or ___ = 0.

Example 1 *Use the zero-product property*

Solve $(x - 5)(x + 4) = 0$.

Solution

$$(x - 5)(x + 4) = 0 \qquad \text{Write original equation.}$$

___ = 0 *or* ___ = 0 _____ property

$x =$ ___ *or* $x =$ ___ Solve for x.

The solutions of the equation are _____.

CHECK Substitute each solution into the original equation to check.

$(\underline{} - 5)(\underline{} + 4) \overset{?}{=} 0 \qquad (\underline{} - 5)(\underline{} + 4) \overset{?}{=} 0$

$\underline{} \overset{?}{=} 0 \qquad\qquad\qquad \underline{} \overset{?}{=} 0$

$\underline{} = 0 \qquad\qquad\qquad\quad \underline{} = 0$

Example 2 *Find the greatest common monomial factor*

Factor out the greatest common monomial factor.

a. $16x + 40y$ **b.** $6x^2 + 30x^3$

Solution

a. The GCF of 16 and 40 is ____. The variables x and y have _____. So, the greatest common monomial factor of the terms is ____.

$16x + 40y =$ _____

b. The GCF of 6 and 30 is ____. The GCF of x^2 and x^3 is _____. So, the greatest common monomial factor of the terms is _____.

$6x^2 + 30x^3 =$ _____

Example 3 *Solve an equation by factoring*

Solve the equation.

a. $3x^2 + 15x = 0$ Original equation

     _____ $= 0$ Factor left side.

     ____ $= 0$ or _____ $= 0$ Zero-product property

       $x =$ ___ or $x =$ _____   Solve for x.

The solutions of the equation are _____.

b. $9b^2 = 24b$ Original equation

     _____ $= 0$ Subtract _____ from each side.

     _____ $= 0$ Factor left side.

     ____ $= 0$ or _____ $= 0$ Zero-product property

       $b =$ ___ or $b =$ _____   Solve for b.

The solutions of the equation are _____.

> To use the zero-product property, you must write the equation so that one side is 0. For this reason, _____ must be subtracted from each side of the equation.

✅ *Checkpoint* **Solve the equation.**

1. $(x + 6)(x - 3) = 0$

---

2. $(x - 8)(x - 5) = 0$

✅ *Checkpoint* **Factor out the greatest common monomial factor.**

3. $10x^2 - 24y^2$

---

4. $3t^6 + 8t^4$

> The vertical motion model takes into account the effect of gravity but ignores other, less significant, factors such as air resistance.

VERTICAL MOTION MODEL

The height h (in feet) of a projectile can be modeled by

$$h = -16t^2 + vt + s$$

where t is the _____ (in seconds) the object has been in the air, v is the _____ (in feet per second), and s is the _____ (in feet).

Example 4   *Solve a multi-step problem*

Fountain A fountain sprays water into the air with an initial vertical velocity of 20 feet per second. After how many seconds does it land on the ground?

Solution

Step 1 Write a model for the water's height above ground.

$$h = -16t^2 + vt + s \qquad \text{Vertical motion model}$$

$$h = -16t^2 + \underline{\quad}t + \underline{\quad} \qquad v = \underline{\quad} \text{ and } s = \underline{\quad}$$

$$h = -16t^2 + \underline{\qquad} \qquad \text{Simplify.}$$

Step 2 Substitute ___ for *h*. When the water lands, its height above the ground is ___ feet. Solve for *t*.

$$\underline{\quad} = -16t^2 + \underline{\qquad} \qquad \text{Substitute } \underline{\quad} \text{ for } h.$$

$$\underline{\quad} = \underline{\qquad\qquad} \qquad \text{Factor right side.}$$

$$\underline{\qquad\qquad} \text{ or } \underline{\qquad\qquad} \qquad \text{Zero-product property}$$

$$\underline{\qquad} \text{ or } \underline{\qquad} \qquad \text{Solve for } t.$$

> The solution $t = 0$ means that before the water is sprayed, its height above the ground is 0 feet.

The water lands on the ground _____ seconds after it is sprayed.

✔ *Checkpoint* **Complete the following exercises.**

5. Solve $d^2 - 7d = 0$.	**6.** Solve $8b^2 = 2b$.

7. What If? In Example 4, suppose the initial vertical velocity is 18 feet per second. After how many seconds does the water land on the ground?

Homework

9.5 Factor $x^2 + bx + c$

Goal • Factor trinomials of the form $x^2 + bx + c$.

Your Notes

FACTORING $x^2 + bx + c$

Algebra

$x^2 + bx + c = (x + p)(x + q)$ provided _____ = b
and _____ = c.

Example

$x^2 + 6x + 5 = ($_____$)($_____$)$ because _____ = 6
and _____ = 5.

Example 1 *Factor when b and c are positive*

Factor $x^2 + 10x + 16$.

Solution

Find two _____ factors of _____ whose sum is _____.
Make an organized list.

Factors of _____	Sum of factors
16, _____	16 + _____ = _____
8, _____	8 + _____ = _____
4, _____	4 + _____ = _____

The factors 8 and ____ have a sum of _____, so they are
the correct values of *p* and *q*.

$x^2 + 10x + 16 = (x + 8)($_____$)$

CHECK

$(x + 8)($_____$) = $ _____   **Multiply.**

$= $ _____   **Simplify.**

Example 2 **Factor when b is negative and c is positive**

Factor $a^2 - 5a + 6$.

Solution

Because b is negative and c is positive, p and q must _____.

Factors of ___	Sum of factors
_____	____ + (____) = ____
_____	____ + (____) = ____

$a^2 - 5a + 6 = ($_____$)($_____$)$

Example 3 **Factor when b is positive and c is negative**

Factor $y^2 + 3y - 10$.

Solution

Because c is negative, p and q must _____ _____.

Factors of _____	Sum of factors
−10, ____	−10 + ____ = ____
10, _____	10 + _____ = ____
−5, ____	−5 + ____ = ____
5, _____	5 + _____ = ____

$y^2 + 3y - 10 = ($_____$)($_____$)$

✔ **Checkpoint** **Factor the trinomial.**

1. $x + 7x + 12$	**2.** $x + 9x + 8$

✅ **Checkpoint** **Factor the trinomial.**

3. $x + 12x + 27$	**4.** $x^2 - 9x + 20$
5. $y^2 + 4y - 21$	**6.** $z^2 + 2z - 24$

Example 4 **Solve a polynomial equation**

Solve the equation $x^2 + 7x = 18$.

$x^2 + 7x = 18$	Write original equation.
$x^2 + 7x -$ _____ $= 0$	Subtract _____ from each side.
_____ $= 0$	Factor left side.
_____ *or* _____	Zero-product property
_____ *or* _____	Solve for x.

The solutions of the equation are _____ .

Example 5 *Solve a multi-step problem*

Dimensions The bandage shown has an area of 16 square centimeters. Find the width of the bandage.

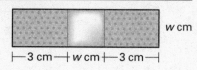

$\vdash$ 3 cm $\dashv$ w cm $\vdash$ 3 cm $\dashv$

Solution

Step 1 Write an equation using the fact that the area of the bandage is 16 square centimeters.

$A = \ell \cdot w$		Formula for area
_____ = _____ $\cdot$ w		Substitute values.
$0 =$ _____		Simplify.

Step 2 Solve the equation for w.

$0 =$ _____		Write equation.
$0 =$ _____		Factor right side.
_____ *or* _____		Zero-product property
_____ *or* _____		Solve for w.

The bandage cannot have a negative width, so the width is _____ .

✔ *Checkpoint* **Complete the following exercises.**

7. Solve the equation $s^2 - 12s = 13$.

Homework

8. What If? In Example 5, suppose the area of the bandage is 27 square centimeters. What is the width?

9.6 Factor $ax^2 + bx + c$

Goal • Factor trinomials of the form $ax^2 + bx + c$.

Example 1 *Factor when b is negative and c is positive*

Factor $2x^2 - 11x + 5$.

Solution

Because b is negative and c is positive, both factors of c must be _____. You must consider the _____ of the factors of 5, because the x-terms of the possible factorizations are different.

Factors of 2	Factors of 5	Possible factorization	Middle term when multiplied
1, 2	-1, ____	$(x - 1)(2x$____$)$	____ $- 2x =$ ____
1, 2	-5, ____	$(x - 5)(2x$____$)$	____ $- 10x =$ ____

$2x^2 - 11x + 5 = (x -$ ___$)(2x$____$)$

Example 2 *Factor when b is positive and c is negative*

Factor $5n^2 + 2n - 3$.

Solution

Because b is positive and c is negative, the factors of c have _____.

Factors of 5	Factors of -3	Possible factorization	Middle term when multiplied
1, 5	1, ____	$(n + 1)(5n$____$)$	_____
1, 5	-1, ___	$(n - 1)(5n$____$)$	_____
1, 5	3, ____	$(n + 3)(5n$____$)$	_____
1, 5	-3, ___	$(n - 3)(5n$____$)$	_____

$5n^2 + 2n - 3 = (n$_____$)(5n$_____$)$

✓ Checkpoint Factor the trinomial.

1. $3x^2 - 5x + 2$	2. $2m^2 + m - 21$

Example 3 *Factor when a is negative*

Factor $-4x^2 + 4x + 3$.

Solution

Step 1 Factor _____ from each term of the trinomial.

$$-4x^2 + 4x + 3 = \underline{\quad}(\underline{\qquad\qquad})$$

Step 2 Factor the trinomial _____. Because b and c are both _____, the factors of c must have _____.

Factors of 4	Factors of −3	Possible factorization	Middle term when multiplied
1, 4	1, _____	$(x + 1)(4x$_____$)$	_____
1, 4	3, _____	$(x + 3)(4x$_____$)$	_____
1, 4	−1, ___	$(x - 1)(4x$_____$)$	_____
1, 4	−3, ___	$(x - 3)(4x$_____$)$	_____
2, 2	1, _____	$(2x + 1)(2x$_____$)$	_____
2, 2	−1, ___	$(2x - 1)(2x$_____$)$	_____

> Remember to include the _____ that you factored out in Step 1.

$$-4x^2 + 4x + 3 = \underline{\qquad\qquad\qquad}$$

✓ Checkpoint Complete the following exercise.

3. Factor $-2y^2 - 11y - 5$.

Example 4 *Write and solve a polynomial equation*

Tennis An athlete hits a tennis ball at an initial height of 8 feet and with an initial vertical velocity of 62 feet per second.

a. Write an equation that gives the height (in feet) of the ball as a function of the time (in seconds) since it left the racket.

b. After how many seconds does the ball hit the ground?

Solution

a. Use the _____ to write an equation for the height h (in feet) of the ball.

$h = -16t^2 + vt + s$ _____

_____

$h = -16t^2 +$ ____ $t +$ ____ $v =$ ____ and $s =$ ____

b. To find the number of seconds that pass before the ball lands, find the value of t for which the height of the ball is ____. Substitute ____ for h and solve the equation for t.

____ $= -16t^2 +$ ____ $t +$ ____   Substitute ____ for h.

____ $=$ ____ (_____)   Factor out ____.

____ $=$ ____ (_____)(_____)   Factor the trinomial.

_____ or _____   Zero-product property

_____ or _____   Solve for t.

A negative solution does not make sense in this situation. The tennis ball hits the ground after _____.

✔ *Checkpoint* **Complete the following exercise.**

4. **What If?** In Example 4, suppose another athlete hits the tennis ball with an initial vertical velocity of 20 feet per second from a height of 6 feet. After how many seconds does the ball hit the ground?

9.7 Factor Special Products

Goal • Factor special products.

VOCABULARY

Perfect square trinomial

DIFFERENCE OF TWO SQUARES PATTERN

Algebra

$a^2 - b^2 = (a + b)(\underline{\hspace{2cm}})$

Example

$9x^2 - 4 = (3x)^2 - 2^2 = (\underline{\hspace{1.5cm}})(\underline{\hspace{1.5cm}})$

Example 1   *Factor the differences of two squares*

Factor the polynomial.

a. $z^2 - 81 = z^2 - \underline{\hspace{0.5cm}}^2$

        $= (z + \underline{\hspace{0.5cm}})(z - \underline{\hspace{0.5cm}})$

b. $16x^2 - 9 = (\underline{\hspace{0.5cm}})^2 - \underline{\hspace{0.5cm}}^2$

         $= (\underline{\hspace{0.5cm}} + \underline{\hspace{0.5cm}})(\underline{\hspace{0.5cm}} - \underline{\hspace{0.5cm}})$

c. $a^2 - 25b^2 = a^2 - (\underline{\hspace{0.5cm}})^2$

         $= (a + \underline{\hspace{0.75cm}})(a - \underline{\hspace{0.75cm}})$

d. $4 - 16n^2 = \underline{\hspace{0.5cm}}(\underline{\hspace{0.5cm}} - \underline{\hspace{0.75cm}})$

         $= \underline{\hspace{0.5cm}}[(\underline{\hspace{0.5cm}})^2 - (\underline{\hspace{0.5cm}})^2]$

         $= \underline{\hspace{0.5cm}}(\underline{\hspace{0.5cm}} + \underline{\hspace{0.5cm}})(\underline{\hspace{0.5cm}} - \underline{\hspace{0.5cm}})$

✓ **Checkpoint** Factor the polynomial.

1. $x^2 - 100$	2. $49y^2 - 25$
3. $c^2 - 9d^2$	4. $45 - 80m^2$

PERFECT SQUARE TRINOMIAL PATTERN

Algebra

$a^2 + 2ab + b^2 = (\underline{\hspace{1.5cm}})^2$

$a^2 - 2ab + b^2 = (\underline{\hspace{1.5cm}})^2$

Example

$x^2 + 8x + 16 = x^2 + 2(x \cdot 4) + 4^2 = (\underline{\hspace{1.5cm}})^2$

$x^2 - 6x + 9 = x^2 - 2(x \cdot 3) + 3^2 = (\underline{\hspace{1.5cm}})^2$

Example 2 *Factor perfect square trinomials*

Factor the polynomial.

a. $x^2 - 16x + 64 = x^2 - 2(\underline{\hspace{1.5cm}}) - \underline{\hspace{0.5cm}}^2$

$\qquad\qquad\qquad = (\underline{\hspace{1.5cm}})^2$

b. $4y^2 - 12y + 9 = (\underline{\hspace{0.8cm}})^2 - 2(\underline{\hspace{1.2cm}}) + \underline{\hspace{0.5cm}}^2$

$\qquad\qquad\qquad = (\underline{\hspace{1.5cm}})^2$

c. $9s^2 + 6st + t^2 = (\underline{\hspace{0.8cm}})^2 + 2(\underline{\hspace{1.2cm}}) + \underline{\hspace{0.5cm}}^2$

$\qquad\qquad\qquad = (\underline{\hspace{1.5cm}})^2$

d. $-3z^2 + 24z - 48 = \underline{\hspace{1cm}}(z^2 - 8z + 16)$

$\qquad\qquad\qquad = \underline{\hspace{1cm}}[z^2 - 2(\underline{\hspace{1cm}}) + \underline{\hspace{0.5cm}}^2]$

$\qquad\qquad\qquad = \underline{\hspace{1cm}}(\underline{\hspace{1.2cm}})^2$

✔ **Checkpoint** **Factor the polynomial.**

5. $x^2 + 14x + 49$	**6.** $9y^2 - 6y + 1$
7. $16x^2 - 40xy + 25y^2$	**8.** $-5r^2 - 20r - 20$

Example 3 *Solve a polynomial equation*

Solve the equation $x^2 + x + \frac{1}{4} = 0$.

$$x^2 + x + \frac{1}{4} = 0 \qquad \text{Write original equation.}$$

$$\underline{\hspace{3cm}} = 0 \qquad \text{Multiply each side by } \underline{\hspace{0.5cm}}.$$

$$\underline{\hspace{3.5cm}} = 0 \qquad \text{Write left side as } a^2 + 2ab + b^2.$$

$$\underline{\hspace{2cm}} = 0 \qquad \text{Perfect square trinomial pattern}$$

$$\underline{\hspace{2cm}} = 0 \qquad \text{Zero-product property}$$

$$x = \underline{\hspace{1cm}} \qquad \text{Solve for } x.$$

> This equation has two identical solutions, because it has two identical factors.

Example 4 *Solve a vertical motion problem*

Falling Object A brick falls off of a building from a height of 144 feet. After how many seconds does the brick land on the ground?

Solution

Use the vertical motion model. The brick fell, so its initial vertical velocity is ___. Find the value of time t (in seconds) for which the height h (in feet) is ___.

$$h = \underline{\hspace{3cm}} \qquad \text{Vertical motion model}$$

$$\underline{\hspace{0.5cm}} = \underline{\hspace{3cm}} \qquad \text{Substitute values.}$$

$$\underline{\hspace{0.5cm}} = \underline{\hspace{1cm}}(\underline{\hspace{1.5cm}}) \qquad \text{Factor out } \underline{\hspace{1cm}}.$$

$$\underline{\hspace{0.5cm}} = \underline{\hspace{1cm}}(\underline{\hspace{1cm}})(\underline{\hspace{1cm}}) \qquad \text{Difference of two squares}$$

$$\underline{\hspace{2cm}} \quad or \quad \underline{\hspace{2cm}} \qquad \text{Zero-product property}$$

$$\underline{\hspace{2cm}} \quad or \quad \underline{\hspace{1.5cm}} \qquad \text{Solve for } t.$$

The brick lands on the ground _____ after it falls.

✔ **Checkpoint** Solve the equation.

9. $m^2 - 8m + 16 = 0$

10. $w^2 + 16w + 64 = 0$

11. $t^2 - 121 = 0$

✔ **Checkpoint** Complete the following exercise.

12. What If? In Example 4, suppose the brick falls from a height of $\frac{225}{4}$ feet. After how many seconds does the brick lands on the ground?

Homework

9.8 Factor Polynomials Completely

Goal • Factor polynomials completely.

Your Notes

VOCABULARY

Factor by grouping _____

_____

Factor completely

Example 1 *Factor out a common binomial*

Factor the expression.

a. $3x(x + 2) - 2(x + 2)$ b. $y^2(y - 4) + 3(4 - y)$

Solution

a. $3x(x + 2) - 2(x + 2) = (x + 2)(\underline{})$

b. The binomials $y - 4$ and $4 - y$ are _____. Factor
   _____ from $4 - y$ to obtain a common binomial factor.

   $y^2(y - 4) + 3(4 - y) = y^2(y - 4)\underline{}$

   $ = (y - 4)\underline{}$

Example 2 *Factor by grouping*

Factor the expression.

a. $y^3 + 7y^2 + 2y + 14$ b. $y^2 + 2y + yx + 2x$

Solution

a. $y^3 + 7y^2 + 2y + 14 = (\underline{}) + (\underline{})$

   $ = \underline{}(\underline{}) + \underline{}(\underline{})$

   $ = (\underline{})(\underline{})$

> Remember that you can check a factorization by multiplying the factors.

b. $y^2 + 2y + yx + 2x = (\underline{}) + (\underline{})$

   $ = \underline{}(\underline{}) + \underline{}(\underline{})$

   $ = (\underline{})(\underline{})$

Example 3   *Factor by grouping*

Factor $x^3 - 12 + 3x - 4x^2$.

Solution

The terms x^3 and -12 have no common factor. Use the _____ to rearrange the terms so that you can group terms with a common factor.

$x^3 - 12 + 3x - 4x^2 =$ _____

$=$ _____

$=$ _____

$=$ _____

✔ *Checkpoint* **Factor the expression.**

1. $5z(z - 6) + 4(z - 6)$	**2.** $2y^2(y - 1) + 7(1 - y)$
3. $x^3 - 4x^2 + 5x - 20$	**4.** $n^3 + 48 + 6n + 8n^2$

GUIDELINES FOR FACTORING POLYNOMIALS COMPLETELY

To factor a polynomial completely, you should try each of these steps.

1. Factor out the _____ common monomial factor.

2. Look for a difference of two squares or a _____ _____.

3. Factor a trinomial of the form $ax^2 + bx + c$ into a product of _____ factors.

4. Factor a polynomial with four terms by _____.

Example 4 *Factor completely*

Factor the polynomial completely.

a. $x^2 + 3x - 1$

b. $3r^3 - 21r^2 + 30r$

c. $9d^4 - 4d^2$

Solution

a. The terms of the polynomial have no common monomial factor. Also, there are no factors of _____ that have a sum of ____. This polynomial _____ be factored.

b. $3r^3 - 21r^2 + 30r =$ _____

   $=$ _____

c. $9d^4 - 4d^2 =$ _____

   $=$ _____

Example 5 *Solve a polynomial equation*

Solve $5x^3 - 25x^2 = -30x$.

Solution

$$5x^3 - 25x^2 = -30x$$
Write original equation.

$$5x^3 - 25x^2 \underline{} 30x = 0$$
_____ $30x$ to each side.

$$\underline{} = 0$$
Factor out ____.

$$\underline{} = 0$$
Factor trinomial.

_____ or _____ or _____
Zero-product property

$x =$ ___ $x =$ ___ $x =$ ___
Solve for x.

> Remember that you can check your answers by substituting each solution for x in the original equation.

Example 6   *Solve a multi-step problem*

Volume A crate in the shape of a rectangular prism has a volume of 180 cubic feet. The crate has a width of w feet, a length of $(9 - w)$ feet, and a height of $(w + 4)$ feet. The length is more than half the width. Find the crate's length, width, and height.

Solution

Step 1 **Write** and solve an equation for w.

$$\text{Volume} = \underline{\hspace{2cm}} \cdot \underline{\hspace{2cm}} \cdot \underline{\hspace{2cm}}$$

$$\underline{\hspace{1cm}} = \underline{\hspace{3cm}}$$

$$0 = \underline{\hspace{4cm}}$$

$$0 = \underline{\hspace{4cm}}$$

$$0 = \underline{\hspace{3.5cm}}$$

$$0 = \underline{\hspace{3.5cm}}$$

$$0 = \underline{\hspace{4cm}}$$

$$\underline{\hspace{1.5cm}} = 0 \ or \ \underline{\hspace{1.5cm}} = 0 \ or \ \underline{\hspace{1.5cm}} = 0$$

$$w = \underline{\hspace{0.5cm}} \qquad w = \underline{\hspace{0.5cm}} \qquad w = \underline{\hspace{0.7cm}}$$

Step 2 **Choose** the solution that is the correct value for w. Disregard _____, because the width cannot be _____.

You know that the length is more than half the width. Test the solutions _____ in the length expression.

Length = _____ = ___ or
Length = _____ = ___.

The solution ___ gives a length of ___ feet, which is more than half the width.

Step 3 **Find** the height.

Height = _____ = _____ = ___.

The width is _____, the length is _____, and the height is _____.

✅ *Checkpoint* **Factor the polynomial.**

5. $-2x^3 + 6x^2 + 108x$

---

6. $12y^4 - 75y^2$

✅ *Checkpoint* **Complete the following exercises.**

7. Solve $2x^3 + 2x^2 = 40x$.

---

8. **What If?** A box in the shape of a rectangular prism has a volume of 180 cubic feet. The box has a length of x feet, a width of $(x + 9)$ feet, and a height of $(x - 4)$ feet. Find the dimensions of the box.

Homework

Words to Review

Give an example of the vocabulary word.

Monomial	Degree of a monomial
Polynomial	Degree of a polynomial
Leading coefficient	Binomial
Trinomial	Roots
Vertical motion model	Perfect square trinomial
Factor by grouping	Factor completely

Review your notes and Chapter 9 by using the Chapter Review on pages 616–620 of your textbook.

10.1 Graph $y = ax^2 + c$

Goal • Graph simple quadratic functions.

Your Notes

VOCABULARY

Quadratic function

_____

Parabola

_____

Parent quadratic function

_____

Vertex

_____

Axis of Symmetry

PARENT QUADRATIC FUNCTION

The most basic quadratic function in the family of quadratic functions, called the _____ _____, is $y = x^2$. The graph is shown below.

The line that passes through the vertex and divides the parabola into two symmetric parts is called the _____ _____. The axis of symmetry for the graph of $y = x^2$ is the y-axis, _____.

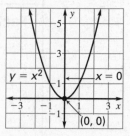

$y = x^2$ $x = 0$

$(0, 0)$

The lowest or highest point on the parabola is the _____. The vertex of the graph of $y = x^2$ is (____, ____).

Example 1 *Graph $y = ax^2$ where $|a| < 1$*

Graph $y = \frac{1}{2}x^2$. Compare the graph with the graph of $y = x^2$.

Solution

Step 1 Make a table of values for $y = \frac{1}{2}x^2$.

x	-4	-2	0	2	4
y	___	___	___	___	___

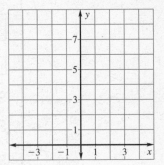

Step 2 _____ the points from the table.

Step 3 Draw a _____ through the points.

Step 4 Compare the graphs of $y = \frac{1}{2}x^2$ and $y = x^2$. Both graphs have the same vertex, (___, ___), and axis of symmetry, _____. However, the graph of $y = \frac{1}{2}x^2$ is _____ than the graph of $y = x^2$. This is because the graph of $y = \frac{1}{2}x^2$ is a vertical _____ (by a factor of ___) of the graph of $y = x^2$.

✔ **Checkpoint Graph the function. Compare the graph with the graph of $y = x^2$.**

1. $y = -5x^2$

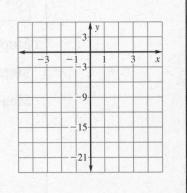

Example 2   *Graph $y = x^2 + c$*

Graph $y = x^2 - 2$. Compare the graph with the graph of $y = x^2$.

Step 1 Make a table of values for
$y = x^2 - 2$.

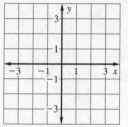

x	−2	−1	0	1	2
y	___	___	___	___	___

Step 2 _____ the points from the table.

Step 3 Draw a _____ through the points.

Step 4 Compare the graphs of $y = x^2 - 2$ and $y = x^2$.
Both graphs open ____ and have the same axis of
symmetry, _____. However, the vertex of the
graph of $y = x^2 - 2$, (___ , ____), is different than
the vertex of the graph of $y = x^2$, (___ , ___),
because the graph of $y = x^2 - 2$ is a _____
_____ (of ___ units _____) of the graph
of $y = x^2$.

Example 3   *Graph $y = ax^2 + c$*

**Graph $y = -3x^2 + 3$. Compare the graph with the
graph of $y = x^2$.**

Step 1 Make a table of values for
$y = -3x^2 + 3$.

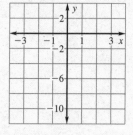

x	−2	−1	0	1	2
y	___	___	___	___	___

Step 2 _____ the points from the table.

Step 3 Draw a _____ through the points.

Step 4 Compare the graphs. Both graphs have the
same axis of symmetry. However, the graph of
$y = -3x^2 + 3$ is _____ and has a _____
vertex than the graph of $y = x^2$ because the graph
of $y = -3x^2 + 3$ is a _____ and
a _____ of the graph of $y = x^2$.

✓ *Checkpoint* **Graph the function. Compare the graph with the graph of $y = x^2$.**

2. $y = \frac{1}{4}x^2 - 6$

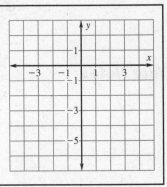

Compared with the graph of $y = x^2$, the graph of $y = ax^2$ is:

$y = ax^2, a > 0$

- a vertical _____ if $a > 1$,

- a vertical _____ if $0 < a < 1$.

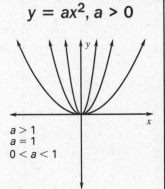

$a > 1$
$a = 1$
$0 < a < 1$

Compared with the graph of $y = x^2$, the graph of $y = ax^2$ is:

$y = ax^2, a < 0$

- a vertical _____ and a _____ in the x-axis if $a < -1$,

- a vertical _____ and a _____ in the x-axis if $-1 < a < 0$.

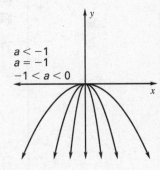

$a < -1$
$a = -1$
$-1 < a < 0$

Compared with the graph of $y = x^2$, the graph of $y = x^2 + c$ is:

$y = x^2 + c$

- an _____ vertical translation if $c > 0$,

- a _____ vertical translation if $c < 0$.

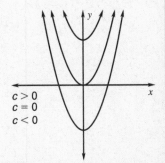

$c > 0$
$c = 0$
$c < 0$

Homework

Graph $y = ax^2 + bx + c$

Goal • Graph general quadratic functions.

VOCABULARY

Minimum value

Maximum value

PROPERTIES OF THE GRAPH OF A QUADRATIC FUNCTION

The graph of $y = ax^2 + bx + c$ is a parabola that:

• opens _____ if $a > 0$ and opens _____ if $a < 0$.

• is narrower than the graph of $y = x^2$ if $|a|$ ___ 1 and wider if $|a|$ ___ 1.

• has an axis of symmetry of

  $x = $ _____ .

• has a vertex with an

  x-coordinate of _____ .

• has a y-intercept of ___ .
  So, the point (___ , ___) is
  on the parabola.

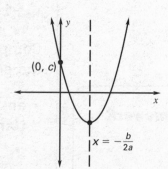

Example 1   *Graph* $y = ax^2 + bx + c$

Graph $y = -x^2 + 4x - 1$.

Step 1 **Determine** whether the parabola opens up or down. Because a ____ 0, the parabola opens _____.

Step 2 **Find** and draw the axis of symmetry:

$$x = -\frac{b}{2a} = \underline{\hspace{2cm}} = \underline{\hspace{1cm}}.$$

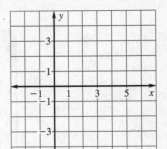

Step 3 **Find** and plot the vertex. The x-coordinate of the vertex is ____, or ____.

To find the y-coordinate, substitute ____ for x in the function and simplify.

$$y = -(\underline{\hspace{0.7cm}})^2 + 4(\underline{\hspace{0.7cm}}) - 1 = 3$$

So, the vertex is (____, ____).

Step 4 **Plot** two points. Choose two x-values less than the x-coordinate of the vertex. Then find the corresponding y-values.

x	1	0
y	___	___

Step 5 _____ the points plotted in Step 4 in the axis of symmetry.

Step 6 **Draw** a _____ through the plotted points.

✔ **Checkpoint** Complete the following exercise.

1. Graph the function $y = 4x^2 + 8x + 3$. Label the vertex and axis of symmetry.

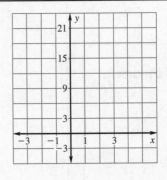

MINIMUM AND MAXIMUM VALUES

For $y = ax^2 + bx + c$, the y-coordinate of the vertex is the _____ value of the function if a ____ 0 and the _____ value of the function if a ____ 0.

Example 2   *Find the minimum or maximum value*

Tell whether the function $f(x) = 5x^2 - 20x + 17$ has a *minimum value* or a *maximum value*. Then find the minimum or maximum value.

Solution

Because $a =$ ____ and _____, the parabola opens _____ and the function has a _____ value. To find the _____ value, find the _____.

$x = -\dfrac{b}{2a} =$ _____ $=$ ____   The x-coordinate is $-\dfrac{b}{2a}$.

$f(\_\_\_) = 5(\_\_\_)^2 - 20(\_\_\_) + 17$ Substitute ____ for x.

$\quad = $ ____   Simplify.

The _____ value of the function is _____.

✔ *Checkpoint* Complete the following exercise.

---

2. Tell whether the function $f(x) = -\dfrac{1}{2}x^2 + 6x + 8$ has a *minimum value* or a *maximum value*. Then find the minimum or maximum value.

Homework

10.3 Solve Quadratic Equations by Graphing

Goal • Solve quadratic equations by graphing.

VOCABULARY

Quadratic equation

Example 1 Solve a quadratic equation having two solutions

Solve $-x^2 + 2x = -8$ by graphing.

Step 1 Write the equation in _____.

$$-x^2 + 2x = -8$$ Write original equation.

$$-x^2 + 2x + 8 = \underline{}$$ Add ___ to each side.

Step 2 Graph the function $y = -x^2 + 2x + 8$.
The x-intercepts are _____ and ___.

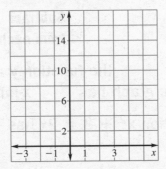

The solutions of the equation $-x^2 + 2x = -8$ are _____ and ___.

CHECK You can check _____ and ___ in the original equation.

$$-x^2 + 2x = -8 \qquad\qquad -x^2 + 2x = -8$$

$$-(\underline{})^2 + 2(\underline{}) \stackrel{?}{=} -8 \qquad -(\underline{})^2 + 2(\underline{}) \stackrel{?}{=} -8$$

$$\underline{} = \underline{} \qquad\qquad \underline{} = \underline{}$$

Example 2 *Solve a quadratic equation having one solution*

Solve $x^2 - 4x = -4$ by graphing.

Step 1 Write the equation in standard form.

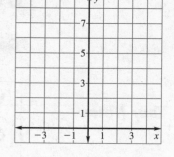

$x^2 - 4x = -4$ Write original equation.

$x^2 - 4x + 4 =$ ___   Add ___ to each side.

Step 2 _____ the function $y = x^2 - 4x + 4$. The x-intercept is ___.

The solution of the equation $x^2 - 4x = -4$ is ___.

Example 3 *Solve a quadratic equation having no solution*

Solve $x^2 + 8 = 2x$ by graphing.

Step 1 Write the equation in standard form.

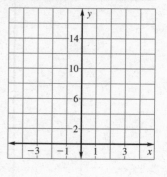

$x^2 + 8 = 2x$ Write original equation.

_____   Subtract ___ from each side.

Step 2 _____ the function $y =$ _____. The graph has ___ x-intercepts.

The equation $x^2 + 8 = 2x$ has _____.

✔ *Checkpoint* **Complete the following exercise.**

1. Solve $x^2 - 6 = -5x$ by graphing.

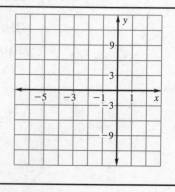

NUMBER OF SOLUTIONS OF A QUADRATIC EQUATION

A quadratic equation has two solutions if the graph of its related function has _____.

A quadratic equation has one solution if the graph of its related function has _____.

A quadratic equation has no solution if the graph of its related function has _____.

Example 4   *Find the zeros of a quadratic function*

Find the zeros of $f(x) = -x^2 - 8x - 7$.

Graph the function
$f(x) = -x^2 - 8x - 7$. The
x-intercepts are _____ and _____.

The zeros of the function are
_____ and _____.

CHECK   Substitute _____ and
_____ in the original function.

$f(\_\_\_) = -(\_\_\_)^2 - 8(\_\_\_) - 7 = \_\_\_$

$f(\_\_\_) = -(\_\_\_)^2 - 8(\_\_\_) - 7 = \_\_\_$

RELATING SOLUTIONS OF EQUATIONS, x-INTERCEPTS OF GRAPHS, AND ZEROS OF FUNCTIONS

Solutions of an Equation

The solutions of the equation $x^2 - 11x + 18$ are ___ and ___.

x-Intercepts of a Graph

The x-intercepts of the graph of
$y = x^2 - 11x + 18$ occur where
$y =$ ___, so the x-intercepts are
___ and ___, as shown.

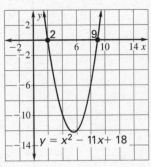

$y = x^2 - 11x + 18$

Zeros of a Function

The zeros of the function
$f(x) = x^2 - 11x + 18$ are the values of x for which
$f(x) =$ ___, so the zeros are ___ and ___.

10.4 Use Square Roots to Solve Quadratic Equations

Goal • Solve a quadratic equation by finding square roots.

Your Notes

SOLVING $x^2 = d$ BY TAKING SQUARE ROOTS

• If $d > 0$, then $x^2 = d$ has _____ solutions: _____.

• If $d = 0$, then $x^2 = d$ has _____ solution: _____.

• If $d < 0$, then $x^2 = d$ has _____ solution.

Example 1   *Solve quadratic equations*

Solve the equation.

a. $z^2 - 5 = 4$ b. $r^2 + 7 = 4$ c. $25k^2 = 9$

Solution

a. $z^2 - 5 = 4$ Write original equation.

   $z^2 =$ _____   Add _____ to each side.

   $z =$ _____   Take square roots of each side.

   $z =$ _____   Simplify. The solutions are _____
                          and _____.

b. $r^2 + 7 = 4$ Write original equation.

   $r^2 =$ _____   Subtract _____ from each side.

Negative real numbers do not have real _____.
So, there is _____.

c. $25k^2 = 9$ Write original equation.

   $k^2 = \underline{}$ Divide each side by _____.

   $k = \underline{}$ Take square roots of each side.

   $k = \underline{}$ Simplify. The solutions are _____

                          and _____.

✓ **Checkpoint** Solve the equation.

1. $3x^2 = 108$	2. $t^2 + 17 = 17$	3. $81p^2 = 4$

Example 2   *Approximate solutions of a quadratic equation*

Solve $4x^2 + 3 = 23$. Round the solutions to the nearest hundredth.

Solution

$4x^2 + 3 = 23$ Write original equation.

$4x^2 = \underline{\hspace{2cm}}$ Subtract ____ from each side.

$x^2 = \underline{\hspace{1cm}}$ Divide each side by ___.

$x = \underline{\hspace{2cm}}$ Take square roots of each side.

$x \approx \underline{\hspace{2cm}}$ Use a calculator. Round to the nearest hundredth.

The solutions are about _____ and _____.

✓ **Checkpoint** Solve the equation. Round the solutions to the nearest hundredth.

4. $2x^2 - 7 = 9$	5. $6g^2 + 1 = 19$

Example 3 *Solve a quadratic equation*

Solve $5(x + 1)^2 = 30$. Round the solutions to the nearest hundredth.

Solution

$5(x + 1)^2 = 30$	Write original equation.
$(x + 1)^2 = $ ___	Divide each side by ___.
$x + 1 = $ _____	Take square roots of each side.
$x = $ _____	Subtract ___ from each side.

The solutions are _____ $\approx$ _____ and

_____ $\approx$ _____.

CHECK To check the solutions, first write the equation so that _____ as follows:

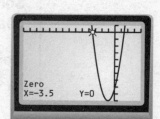

$5(x + 1)^2 - 30 = 0$. Then graph the related function $y = 5(x + 1)^2 - 30$. The x-intercepts appear to be about _____ and about _____. So, each solution checks.

✔ *Checkpoint* Solve the equation. Round the solutions to the nearest hundredth, if necessary.

6. $3(m - 4)^2 = 12$	**7.** $4(a - 3)^2 = 32$

Homework

10.5 Solve Quadratic Equations by Completing the Square

Goal • Solve quadratic equations by completing the square.

VOCABULARY

Completing the square

COMPLETING THE SQUARE

Words To complete the square for the expression $x^2 + bx$, add the _____ of the term bx.

Algebra $x^2 + bx + \left(\dfrac{b}{2}\right)^2 = \left(x + \dfrac{b}{2}\right)^2$

Example 1 *Complete the square*

Find the value of c that makes the expression $x^2 - 5x + c$ a perfect square trinomial. Then write the expression as the square of the binomial.

Solution

Step 1 **Find** the value of c. For the expression to be a perfect square trinomial, c needs to be the square of half the coefficient of the term bx.

$c = \left(\dfrac{\boxed{}}{2}\right)^2 = \underline{}$ **Find the square of half the coefficient of bx.**

Step 2 **Write** the expression as a perfect square trinomial. Then write the expression as the square of a binomial.

$x^2 - 5x + c = x^2 - 5x + \underline{}$ **Substitute** _____ **for c.**

$= \underline{}^2$ **Square of a binomial**

✔ *Checkpoint* **Find the value of c that makes the expression a perfect square trinomial. Then write the expression as the square of a binomial.**

1. $x^2 + 7x + c$	2. $x^2 - 6x + c$

Example 2 *Solve a quadratic equation*

Solve $t^2 + 6t = -5$ by completing the square.

Solution

$$t^2 + 6t = -5$$ Write original equation.

$$t^2 + 6t + \underline{\quad} = -5 + \underline{\quad}$$ Add $\left(\underline{\quad}\right)^2$, or ____, to each side.

$$\underline{\hspace{2cm}} = -5 + \underline{\quad}$$ Write left side as the square of a binomial.

$$\underline{\hspace{2cm}} = \underline{\quad}$$ Simplify the right side.

$$\underline{\hspace{2cm}} = \underline{\quad}$$ Take square roots of each side.

$$t = \underline{\hspace{2cm}}$$ Subtract ____ from each side.

The solutions of the equation are _____ **and** _____ **.**

Example 3 *Solve a quadratic equation in standard form*

Solve $4m^2 - 16m + 8 = 0$ by completing the square.

Solution

$4m^2 - 16m + 8 = 0$	Write original equation.
$4m^2 - 16m = \underline{\quad}$	Subtract ___ from each side.
$m^2 - 4m = \underline{\quad}$	Divide each side by ___.
$m^2 - 4m + \underline{\quad} = -2 + \underline{\quad}$	Add $\left(\underline{\quad}\right)^2$, or _____, to each side.
$\underline{\quad\quad} = \underline{\quad}$	Write left side as the square of a binomial.
$\underline{\quad\quad} = \underline{\quad\quad}$	Take square roots of each side.
$m = \underline{\quad\quad}$	Add ___ to each side.

The solutions are _____ ≈ _____ and _____ ≈ _____ .

✔ *Checkpoint* Solve the equation by completing the square. Round your solutions to the nearest hundredth, if necessary.

3. $r^2 - 8r = 9$	4. $5s^2 + 60s + 125 = 0$

Homework

10.6 Solve Quadratic Equations by the Quadratic Formula

Goal • Solve quadratic equations using the quadratic formula.

Your Notes

VOCABULARY

Quadratic formula

THE QUADRATIC FORMULA

The solutions of the quadratic equation

$ax^2 + bx + c = 0$ are $x = \dfrac{-b \pm \sqrt{b^2 - 4ac}}{2a}$ when $a \neq 0$

and $b^2 - 4ac \geq 0$.

Example 1 *Solve a quadratic equation*

Solve $2x^2 - 5 = 3x$.

$$2x^2 - 5 = 3x$$ Write original equation.

_____   Write in standard form.

$x = \dfrac{-b \pm \sqrt{b^2 - 4ac}}{2a}$ **Quadratic formula**

$= \dfrac{-\underline{} \pm \sqrt{\underline{}^2 - 4(\underline{})(\underline{})}}{2(\underline{})}$ **Substitute values in the quadratic formula:** $a =$ _____, $b =$ _____, and $c =$ _____.

$= \dfrac{\underline{} \pm \sqrt{\underline{}}}{\underline{}}$ **Simplify.**

$= \dfrac{\underline{} \pm \underline{}}{\underline{}}$ **Simplify the square root.**

> Check your solution by graphing the related function and finding the *x*-intercepts.

The solutions are $\dfrac{\underline{} + \underline{}}{\underline{}} =$ _____ and $\dfrac{\underline{} - \underline{}}{\underline{}} =$ _____.

Example 2 Use the quadratic formula

Crabbing A crabbing net is thrown from a bridge, which is 35 feet above the water. If the net's initial velocity is 10 feet per second, how long will it take the net to hit the water?

Solution

The net's initial velocity is $v =$ _____ feet per second and the net's initial height is $s =$ _____ feet. The net will hit the water when the height is ___ feet.

$h = -16t^2 + vt + s$ **Vertical motion model**

___ $= -16t^2 +$ ____ $t +$ ____   **Substitute for h, v, and s.**

$$t = \frac{-\underline{} \pm \sqrt{\underline{}^2 - 4(\underline{})(\underline{})}}{2(\underline{})}$$

Substitute values in the quadratic formula:

$a =$ _____,

$b =$ _____, and

$c =$ ____.

$$= \frac{\pm \sqrt{\underline{}}}{\underline{}}$$

Simplify.

The solutions are $\dfrac{\underline{} + \sqrt{\underline{}}}{\underline{}} \approx$ _____ and

$\dfrac{\underline{} - \sqrt{\underline{}}}{\underline{}} \approx$ _____. So, the net will hit the water in about _____ seconds.

> Because time cannot be a negative number, disregard the negative solution.

✔ **Checkpoint** Complete the following exercises.

1. Use the quadratic formula to solve $2x^2 + x = 3$.

2. In Example 2, suppose the net was thrown with an initial velocity of 5 feet per second from a height of 20 feet. How long would it take the net to hit the water?

METHODS FOR SOLVING QUADRATIC EQUATIONS

Methods	When to Use
Factoring	Use when a quadratic equation can be _____ easily.
Graphing	Use when _____ solutions are adequate.
Finding square roots	Use when solving an equation that can be written in the form _____.
Completing the square	Can be used for any quadratic equation $ax^2 + bx + c = 0$ but is simplest to apply when _____ and b is an _____ number.
Quadratic formula	Can be used for _____ quadratic equation.

Example 3 *Choose a solution method*

Tell what method(s) you would use to solve the quadratic equation. *Explain* **your choice(s).**

a. $6x^2 - 11x + 7 = 0$ **b.** $4x^2 - 36 = 0$

Solution

a. The quadratic equation _____ be factored easily and completing the square would result in _____ _____. So, the equation can be solved using the _____.

b. The quadratic equation can be solved using _____ _____ because the equation can be written in the form $x^2 = d$.

✔ *Checkpoint* **Complete the following exercise.**

3. Tell what method(s) you would use to solve $x^2 + 8x = 9$. *Explain* your choices(s).

10.7 Interpret the Discriminant

Goal • Use the value of the discriminant.

Your Notes

VOCABULARY

Discriminant

USING THE DISCRIMINANT OF $ax^2 + bx + c = 0$

Value of the discriminant	Number of solutions	Graph of $y = ax^2 + bx + c$
$b^2 - 4ac > 0$	_____	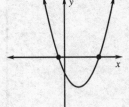
$b^2 - 4ac = 0$	_____	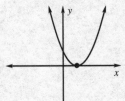
$b^2 - 4ac < 0$	_____	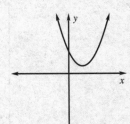

Example 1 *Use the discriminant*

Equation   **Discriminant**
$ax^2 + bx + c = 0$ $b^2 - 4ac$

a. $x^2 - 3x - 2 = 0$ ____^{2} $- 4($___$)($___$) = $ ____

b. $3x^2 + 2 = 0$ ___^{2} $- 4($___$)($___$) = $ _____

c. $2x^2 + 8x + 8 = 0$ ___^{2} $- 4($___$)($___$) = $ ___

Number of solutions

a. _____ b. _____ c. _____

Example 2 *Find the number of solutions*

Tell whether the equation $-2x^2 + 4x = 2$ has *two solutions, one solution,* or *no solution*.

Step 1 Write the equation in _____.

$-2x^2 + 4x = 2$ Write equation.

$-2x^2 + 4x - 2 = 0$ Subtract ____ from each side.

Step 2 Find the value of the _____.

$b^2 - 4ac = $ ___$^2 - 4($_____$)($_____$)$ Substitute _____ for *a*, ____ for *b*, and _____ for *c*.

$= $ ___   Simplify.

The discriminant is ___, so the equation has _____ _____.

✔ *Checkpoint* **Tell whether the equation has *two solutions, one solution,* or *no solution*.**

1. $x^2 + 2x = 1$	**2.** $3x^2 + 7x = -5$
3. $5x^2 - 6 = 0$	**4.** $-x^2 - 9 = 6x$

Example 3 _Find the number of x-intercepts_

Find the number of x-intercepts of the graph of
$y = -x^2 + 3x + 4$.

Solution

Find the _____ of the equation
$0 = -x^2 + 3x + 4$.

$b^2 - 4ac = \underline{}^2 - 4(\underline{})(\underline{})$ **Substitute** _____ **for** _a_,
_____ **for** _b_, **and** _____ **for** _c_.

$= \underline{}$ **Simplify.**

The discriminant is _____, so the equation
has _____. This means that the graph
of $y = -x^2 + 3x + 4$ has _____ x-intercepts.

CHECK You can use a graphing
calculator to check the answer.
Notice that the graph of
$y = -x^2 + 3x + 4$ has _____
intercepts.

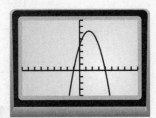

✔ **Checkpoint** Find the number of x-intercepts of the
graph of the function.

5. $y = -x^2 + 3x - 3$	6. $y = x^2 - 4x + 4$

Homework

10.8 Compare Linear, Exponential, and Quadratic Models

Goal • Compare linear, exponential, and quadratic models.

Your Notes

LINEAR, EXPONENTIAL, AND QUADRATIC FUNCTIONS

Linear Function	Exponential Function	Quadratic Function
$y =$ _____	$y =$ _____	$y =$ _____

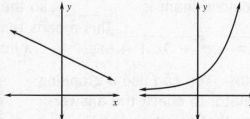
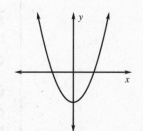

Example 1 *Choose functions using sets of ordered pairs*

Use a graph to tell whether the ordered pairs represent a *linear function*, an *exponential function*, or a *quadratic function*.

a. $(-2, 7)$, $(-1, 1)$, $(0, -1)$, $(1, 1)$, $(2, 7)$

b. $(-2, 4)$, $(-1, 2)$, $(0, 1)$, $\left(1, \frac{1}{2}\right)$, $\left(2, \frac{1}{4}\right)$

c. $(-2, 5)$, $(-1, 3)$, $(0, 1)$, $(1, -1)$, $(2, -3)$

Solution

a.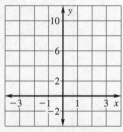

b.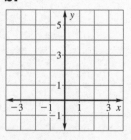

c.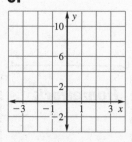

_____ function   _____ function   _____ function

Example 2 *Identify functions using differences or ratios*

Use differences or ratios to tell whether the table of values represents a *linear function*, an *exponential function*, or a *quadratic function*.

a.

x	-2	-1	0	1	2
y	-12	-8	-4	0	4

Differences: ___ ___ ___ ___

The table of values represents _____ function.

b.

x	-2	-1	0	1	2
y	0.25	0.5	1	2	4

Ratios: $\dfrac{\boxed{}}{\boxed{}}$ = ___ ___ ___ ___

The table of values represents _____ function.

✔ *Checkpoint* **Complete the following exercises.**

1. Tell whether the ordered pairs represent a *linear function*, an *exponential function*, or a *quadratic function*: $(-2, -1), (-1, 1), (0, 3), (1, 5), (2, 7)$.

_____

2. Tell whether the table of values represents a *linear function*, an *exponential function*, or a *quadratic function*:

x	-2	-1	0	1	2
y	3	0.75	0	0.75	3

Example 3 *Write an equation for a function*

Tell whether the table of values represents a *linear function*, an *exponential function*, or a *quadratic function*. Then write an equation for the function.

x	−2	−1	0	1	2
y	32	8	2	0.5	0.125

Step 1 Determine which type of function the values in the table represent.

x	−2	−1	0	1	2
y	32	8	2	0.5	0.25

Ratios: $\dfrac{\boxed{}}{\boxed{}}$ = _____ _____ _____ _____

The table of values represents _____ function.

Step 2 Write an equation for the _____ function. The ratio of successive *y*-values is _____, so *b* = _____. Find the value of *a* using the coordinates of a point that lies on the graph, such as (0, 2).

$y = $ _____   Write equation for _____ function.

____ = _____   Substitute _____ for *b*, ____ for *x*, and ____ for *y*.

____ = *a*   Solve for *a*.

The equation is _____.

Homework

✔ *Checkpoint* Complete the following exercise.

3. Write an equation for the function in Checkpoint 2.

Words to Review

Give an example of the vocabulary word.

Quadratic function	Parent quadratic function
Parabola	Vertex
Axis of symmetry	Minimum value
Maximum value	Quadratic equation

Completing the square	Quadratic formula
Discriminant	

Review your notes and Chapter 10 by using the Chapter Review on pages 696–700 of your textbook.

11.1 Graph Square Root Functions

Goal • Graph square root functions.

Your Notes

VOCABULARY

Radical expression

Radical function

Square root function

Parent square root function

PARENT FUNCTION FOR SQUARE ROOT FUNCTIONS

The most basic square root function in the family of all square root functions, called the _____

_____, is y = _____.

The graph of the parent square root function is shown.

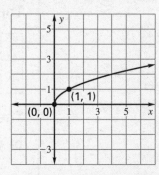

Example 1   *Graph a function of the form y = a√x*

Graph the function $y = -4\sqrt{x}$ and identify its domain and range. Compare the graph with the graph of $y = \sqrt{x}$.

Solution

Step 1 Make a table. Because the square root of a negative number is _____, x must be nonnegative. So, the domain is _____.

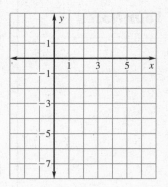

x	0	1	2	3
y	__	__	__	__

Step 2 Plot the points.

Step 3 Draw a _____ through the points. From either the table or the graph, you can see the range of the function is _____.

Step 4 Compare the graph with the graph of $y = \sqrt{x}$. The graph of $y = -4\sqrt{x}$ is vertical _____ (by a factor of ___) and a _____ of the graph $y = \sqrt{x}$.

Example 2   *Graph a function of the form y = √x + k*

Graph the function $y = \sqrt{x} - 2$ and identify its domain and range. Compare the graph with the graph of $y = \sqrt{x}$.

Solution

To graph the function, make a table, then plot and connect the points. The domain is _____.

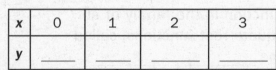

x	0	1	2	3
y	__	__	__	__

The range is _____. The graph of $y = \sqrt{x} - 2$ is a _____ (of ___ units _____) of the graph of $y = \sqrt{x}$.

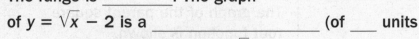

✅ *Checkpoint* **Graph the function and identify its domain and range. Compare the graph with the graph of** $y = \sqrt{x}$.

1. $y = 0.25\sqrt{x}$

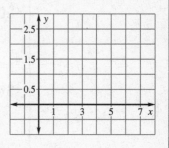

2. $y = \sqrt{x} + 4$

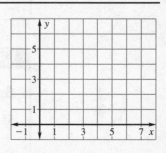

Example 3 *Graph a function of the form* $y = \sqrt{x - h}$

Graph the function $y = \sqrt{x + 5}$ **and identify its domain and range. Compare the graph with the graph of** $y = \sqrt{x}$.

Solution

To graph the function, make a table, then plot and connect the points. To find the domain, find the values of x for which the radicand, $x + 5$, is _____. The domain is _____.

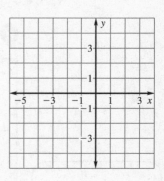

x	-5	-4	-3	-2
y	___	___	___	___

The range is _____. The graph of $y = \sqrt{x + 5}$ is a _____ (of ___ units to the _____) of the graph of $y = \sqrt{x}$.

GRAPHS OF SQUARE ROOT FUNCTIONS

To graph a function of the form $y = a\sqrt{x - h} + k$, you can follow these steps.

Step 1 Sketch the graph of $y = a\sqrt{x}$. The graph of $y = a\sqrt{x}$ starts at the _____ and passes through the point _____.

Step 2 Shift the graph $|h|$ units _____ (to the right if h is _____ and to the left if h is _____) and $|k|$ units _____ (____ if k is positive and _____ if k is negative).

Example 4   *Graph a function of the form $y = a\sqrt{x - h} + k$*

Graph the function $y = 3\sqrt{x - 1} + 2$.

Step 1 Sketch the graph of $y = 3\sqrt{x}$.

Step 2 Shift the graph $|h|$ units horizontally and $|k|$ units vertically. Notice that $h =$ ___ and $k =$ ___. Shift the graph _____ and _____.

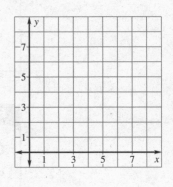

✔ *Checkpoint* **Complete the following exercises.**

3. Graph the function $y = \sqrt{x} - 3$ and identify its domain and range. Compare the graph with the graph of $y = \sqrt{x}$.

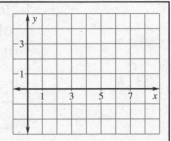

---

4. Identify the domain and range of the function in Example 4.

11.2 Simplify Radical Expressions

Goal • Simplify radical expressions.

Your Notes

VOCABULARY

Simplest form of a radical expression

Rationalizing the denominator

PRODUCT PROPERTY OF RADICALS

Words The square root of a product equals the _____ of the _____ of the factors.

Algebra $\sqrt{ab} = $ _____ • _____ where $a \geq 0$ and $b \geq 0$

Example $\sqrt{9x} = $ _____ • _____ = _____

Example 1 *Use the product property of radicals*

Simplify $\sqrt{12x^2}$.

Solution

$\sqrt{12x^2} = \sqrt{\underline{\quad} \cdot \underline{\quad} \cdot \underline{\quad}}$ **Factor using perfect square factors.**

$= \underline{\quad} \cdot \underline{\quad} \cdot \underline{\quad}$ _____ of radicals

$= \underline{\quad}$ **Simplify.**

Example 2   *Multiply radicals*

a. $\sqrt{8} \cdot \sqrt{2} = \sqrt{\underline{} \cdot \underline{}}$

$= \underline{}$

$= \underline{}$

b. $\sqrt{5x^3 y} \cdot 2\sqrt{x} = \underline{}\sqrt{\underline{} \cdot \underline{}}$

$= \underline{}\sqrt{\underline{}}$

$= \underline{} \cdot \underline{} \cdot \underline{} \cdot \underline{}$

$= \underline{}$

QUOTIENT PROPERTY OF RADICALS

Words The square root of a quotient equals the
_____ of the _____ of the numerator
and denominator.

Algebra $\sqrt{\dfrac{a}{b}} = \dfrac{\boxed{}}{\boxed{}}$ where $a \geq 0$ and $b > 0$

Example $\sqrt{\dfrac{4}{9}} = \dfrac{\boxed{}}{\boxed{}} = \underline{}$

Example 3   *Use the quotient property of radicals*

a. $\sqrt{\dfrac{11}{49}} = \dfrac{\boxed{}}{\boxed{}}$ **Quotient property of radicals**

$= \dfrac{\boxed{}}{\boxed{}}$ **Simplify.**

b. $\sqrt{\dfrac{t^2}{36}} = \dfrac{\boxed{}}{\boxed{}}$ **Quotient property of radicals**

$= \underline{}$ **Simplify.**

✔ **Checkpoint** Simplify the expression.

1. $\sqrt{16z^4}$	2. $4\sqrt{mn} \cdot \sqrt{5m}$	3. $\sqrt{\dfrac{15}{25}}$

Example 4 **Rationalize the denominator**

a. $\dfrac{\sqrt{2}}{\sqrt{5}} = \dfrac{\sqrt{2}}{\sqrt{5}} \cdot \dfrac{\boxed{}}{\boxed{}}$ Multiply by $\dfrac{\sqrt{5}}{\sqrt{5}}$.

$= \dfrac{\boxed{}}{\boxed{}}$ Product property of radicals

$= \dfrac{\boxed{}}{\boxed{}}$ Simplify.

b. $\dfrac{1}{\sqrt{7r}} = \dfrac{1}{\sqrt{7r}} \cdot \dfrac{\sqrt{7r}}{\sqrt{7r}}$ Multiply by $\underline{}$.

$= \dfrac{\boxed{}}{\boxed{}}$ Product property of radicals

$= \dfrac{\boxed{}}{\boxed{}}$ Product property of radicals

$= \underline{}$ Simplify.

Example 5 *Add and subtract radicals*

a. $7\sqrt{5} - \sqrt{11} + 4\sqrt{5}$

= _____ **Commutative property**

= _____ **Distributive property**

= _____ **Simplify.**

b. $2\sqrt{2} - \sqrt{18}$

= _____ **Factor using perfect square factors.**

= _____ **Product property of radicals**

= _____ **Simplify.**

= _____ **Distributive property**

= _____ **Simplify.**

✔ *Checkpoint* **Simplify the expression.**

4. $\dfrac{2}{\sqrt{5y}}$	5. $3\sqrt{11} + 2\sqrt{44}$

Example 6 *Multiply radical expressions*

Multiply $(4 + \sqrt{3})(3 - \sqrt{3})$.

Solution

$(4 + \sqrt{3})(3 - \sqrt{3})$

$= \underline{\quad} + \underline{\qquad} + \underline{\quad} + \underline{\qquad}$ **Multiply.**

$= \underline{\hspace{4cm}}$ **Product property of radicals**

$= \underline{\hspace{3.5cm}}$ **Simplify.**

$= \underline{\hspace{1.5cm}}$ **Simplify.**

✔ *Checkpoint* **Simplify the expression.**

6. $\sqrt{7}(2\sqrt{7} + \sqrt{3})$

7. $(3\sqrt{5} + 7)^2$

8. $(2 + \sqrt{6})(8 - \sqrt{6})$

Homework

11.3 Solve Radical Equations

Goal • Solve radical equations.

Your Notes

VOCABULARY

Radical equation

Extraneous solution

SQUARING BOTH SIDES OF AN EQUATION

Words If two expressions are equal, then their squares are _____.

Algebra If $a = b$, then _____.

Example If $\sqrt{x} = 4$, then _____.

Example 1 *Solve a radical equation*

Solve $3\sqrt{x + 1} - 15 = -6$.

Solution

$3\sqrt{x + 1} - 15 = -6$	Write original equation.
$3\sqrt{x + 1} = \underline{\ \ }$	Add ____ to each side.
$\sqrt{x + 1} = \underline{\ \ }$	Divide each side by ___.
$\underline{\ \ \ \ } = \underline{\ \ }$	Square each side.
$\underline{\ \ \ \ } = \underline{\ \ }$	Simplify.
$x = \underline{\ \ }$	Subtract ____ from each side.

The solution is ___.

> Check the solution by substituting it in the original equation.

✔ **Checkpoint** **Complete the following exercise.**

1. Solve $\sqrt{4x - 19} - 2 = 5$.

Example 2 **Solve an equation with a radical on both sides**

Solve $\sqrt{3x - 3} = \sqrt{2x + 8}$.

Solution

$\sqrt{3x - 3} = \sqrt{2x + 8}$		Write original equation.
_____ = _____		Square each side.
_____ = _____		Simplify.
_____ = ___		Subtract ____ from each side.
$x = $ ___		Add ___ to each side.

The solution is ____.

> To solve a radical equation that contains two radical expressions, be sure that each side of the equation has only one radical expression before squaring each side.

✔ **Checkpoint** **Solve the equation.**

2. $\sqrt{5x - 4} = \sqrt{3x + 20}$	3. $\sqrt{13 - x} = \sqrt{3x - 15}$

Example 3   *Solve an equation with an extraneous solution*

Solve $x = \sqrt{2x + 15}$.

Solution

$$x = \sqrt{2x + 15}$$ Write original equation

$$\underline{\hspace{2em}} = \underline{\hspace{4em}}$$ Square each side.

$$\underline{\hspace{2em}} = \underline{\hspace{3em}}$$ Simplify.

$$\underline{\hspace{5em}} = 0$$ Write in standard form.

$$(\underline{\hspace{3em}})(\underline{\hspace{3em}}) = 0$$ Factor.

$$(\underline{\hspace{3em}}) = 0 \quad or \quad (\underline{\hspace{3em}}) = 0$$

$$x = \underline{\hspace{1em}} \quad or \quad x = \underline{\hspace{2em}}$$

CHECK   Check $\underline{\hspace{1em}}$ and $\underline{\hspace{2em}}$ in the original equation.

$x = \underline{\hspace{1em}}$: $x = \underline{\hspace{1em}}$:

$\underline{\hspace{1em}} \stackrel{?}{=} \sqrt{2(\underline{\hspace{1em}}) + 15}$ $\underline{\hspace{1.5em}} \stackrel{?}{=} \sqrt{2(\underline{\hspace{1.5em}}) + 15}$

$5 = \underline{\hspace{1em}}$ ✓ $-3 = \underline{\hspace{1em}}$ ✗

Because $\underline{\hspace{2em}}$ does not check in the original equation, it is an $\underline{\hspace{6em}}$. The only solution to the equation is $\underline{\hspace{1em}}$.

✓ **Checkpoint** Solve the equation.

4. $\sqrt{20 - x} = x$	5. $\sqrt{7 + 6x} = x$

Homework

11.4 Apply the Pythagorean Theorem and its Converse

Goal • Use the Pythagorean theorem and its converse.

Your Notes

VOCABULARY

Hypotenuse

Legs of a right triangle

Pythagorean theorem

THE PYTHAGOREAN THEOREM

Words If a triangle is a right triangle, then the _____

_____ equals

the _____

_____.

Algebra _____

Example 1 *Use the Pythagorean theorem*

The lengths of the legs of a right triangle are $a = 8$ and $b = 15$. Find c.

Solution

$c^2 = a^2 + b^2$	**Pythagorean theorem**
$c^2 = \_\_\_^2 + \_\_\_^2$	**Substitute ___ for a and ___ for b.**
$c^2 = \_\_\_\_\_$	**Simplify.**
$c = \_\_\_\_$	**Take positive square root of each side.**

The side length of c is _____.

✔ *Checkpoint* **Complete the following exercises.**

1. The lengths of the legs of a right triangle are $a = 7$ and $b = 9$. Find c.

_____

2. The length of a leg of a right triangle is $a = 20$ and the length of the hypotenuse is $c = 52$. Find b.

Example 2   *Use the Pythagorean theorem*

A right triangle has one leg that is 4 inches longer than the other leg. The hypotenuse is $\sqrt{106}$ inches. Find the unknown lengths.

Solution

Sketch a right triangle and label the sides with their lengths. Let x be the length of the shorter leg.

$a^2 + b^2 = c^2$	Pythagorean theorem
$\underline{}^2 + (\underline{})^2 = (\underline{})^2$	Substitute.
$\underline{} + \underline{} = \underline{}$	Simplify.
$\underline{} = 0$	Write in standard form.
$\underline{} = 0$	Factor.
$(\underline{}) = 0$ *or* $(\underline{}) = 0$	Zero-product property
$x = \underline{}$ *or* $x = \underline{}$	Solve for x.

Because length is nonnegative, the solution $x = \underline{}$ does not make sense. The legs have lengths of ___ inches and ___ + 4 = ___ inches.

✓ *Checkpoint* **Complete the following exercise.**

3. A right triangle has one leg that is 2 centimeters shorter than the other leg. The length of the hypotenuse is 10 centimeters. Find the unknown lengths.

CONVERSE OF THE PYTHAGOREAN THEOREM

If a triangle has side lengths a, b, and c such that _____, then the triangle is a _____ triangle.

Example 3 *Determine right triangles*

Tell whether the triangle with the given side lengths is a right triangle.

a. 10, 11, 15

$$10^2 + 11^2 \stackrel{?}{=} 15^2$$

$$\underline{\hspace{1cm}} + \underline{\hspace{1cm}} \stackrel{?}{=} \underline{\hspace{1cm}}$$

$$\underline{\hspace{2cm}}$$

The triangle _____ a right triangle.

b. 3, 4, 5

$$3^2 + 4^2 \stackrel{?}{=} 5^2$$

$$\underline{\hspace{1cm}} + \underline{\hspace{1cm}} \stackrel{?}{=} \underline{\hspace{1cm}}$$

$$\underline{\hspace{2cm}}$$

The triangle _____ a right triangle.

✓ *Checkpoint* **Tell whether the triangle with the given side lengths is a right triangle.**

4. 9, 40, 41	5. 10, 15, 18

6. A triangular mirror has side lengths of 1.2 meters, 1.6 meters, and 2 meters. Is the mirror a right triangle? Explain.

Homework

11.5 Apply the Distance and Midpoint Formulas

Goal • Use the distance and midpoint formulas.

Your Notes

VOCABULARY

Distance formula

Midpoint

Midpoint formula

THE DISTANCE FORMULA

The distance between any two points (x_1, y_1) and (x_2, y_2) is

_____ .

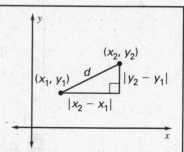

Example 1   *Find the distance between two points*

Find the distance between $(4, -3)$ and $(-7, 2)$.

Let $(x_1, y_1) = (4, -3)$ and $(x_2, y_2) = (-7, 2)$.

$d = \sqrt{(x_2 - x_1)^2 + (y_2 - y_1)^2}$ **Distance formula**

$= \sqrt{(\underline{\quad} - \underline{\quad})^2 + (\underline{\quad} - \underline{\quad})^2}$ **Substitute.**

$= \sqrt{(\underline{\quad})^2 + (\underline{\quad})^2} = \underline{\quad}$ **Simplify.**

The distance between the points is _____ units.

Copyright © McDougal Littell/Houghton Mifflin Company.

Example 2   *Find a missing coordinate*

The distance between (5, *a*) and (9, 6) is $4\sqrt{2}$ units.
Find the value of *a*.

Solution

Use the distance formula with $d = 4\sqrt{2}$. Let
$(x_1, y_1) = (5, a)$ and $(x_2, y_2) = (9, 6)$.

$d = \sqrt{(x_2 - x_1)^2 + (y_2 - y_1)^2}$	Distance formula
$\underline{\hspace{1cm}} = \sqrt{(\underline{\hspace{0.5cm}} - \underline{\hspace{0.5cm}})^2 + (\underline{\hspace{0.5cm}} - \underline{\hspace{0.5cm}})^2}$	Substitute.
$\underline{\hspace{1cm}} = \sqrt{\underline{\hspace{2cm}}}$	Multiply.
$\underline{\hspace{1cm}} = \sqrt{\underline{\hspace{2cm}}}$	Simplify.
$\underline{\hspace{1cm}} = \underline{\hspace{2cm}}$	Square each side.
$0 = \underline{\hspace{2cm}}$	Write in standard form.
$0 = \underline{\hspace{2cm}}$	Factor.
$\underline{\hspace{2cm}} = 0$ *or* $\underline{\hspace{2cm}} = 0$	Zero-product property
$a = \underline{\hspace{1cm}}$ *or* $a = \underline{\hspace{1cm}}$	Solve for *a*.

The value of *a* is $\underline{\hspace{1cm}}$ or $\underline{\hspace{1cm}}$.

✔ *Checkpoint* **Complete the following exercises.**

1. Find the distance between (2, −3) and (5, 1).	**2.** The distance between (−1, 2) and (3, *b*) is $\sqrt{41}$ units. Find the value of *b*.

THE MIDPOINT FORMULA

The midpoint M of the line segment with endpoints $A(x_1, y_1)$ and $B(x_2, y_2)$ is

$$M\left(\underline{\hspace{2cm}}, \underline{\hspace{2cm}} \right).$$

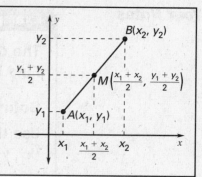

Example 3 *Find the midpoint between two points*

Find the midpoint of the line segment with endpoints $(-3, 7)$ and $(-1, 11)$.

Solution

Let $(x_1, y_1) = (-3, 7)$ and $(x_2, y_2) = (-1, 11)$.

$$\left(\frac{x_1 + x_2}{2}, \frac{y_1 + y_2}{2} \right) = \left(\frac{\boxed{} + \boxed{}}{\boxed{}}, \frac{\boxed{} + \boxed{}}{\boxed{}} \right)$$

$$= (\underline{\hspace{1cm}}, \underline{\hspace{1cm}})$$

The midpoint is $(\underline{\hspace{1cm}}, \underline{\hspace{1cm}})$.

✔ **Checkpoint** Find the midpoint of the line segment with the given endpoints.

3. $(1, -2)$, $(5, -4)$	4. $(5, 12)$, $(13, 8)$

Homework

Words to Review

Give an example of the vocabulary word.

Radical expression	Radical function
Square root function	Parent square root function
Simplest form of a radical expression	Rationalizing the denominator
Radical equation	Extraneous solution
Hypotenuse	Legs of a right triangle

Words to Review

Pythagorean theorem	Distance formula
Midpoint	Midpoint formula

Review your notes and Chapter 11 by using the Chapter Review on pages 754–756 of your textbook.

12.1 Model Inverse Variation

Goal • Write and graph inverse variation equations.

VOCABULARY

Inverse variation

_____

Constant of variation

_____

Hyperbola

_____

Branches of a hyperbola

_____

Asymptotes of a hyperbola

Example 1 *Identify direct and inverse variation*

Tell whether the equation represents *direct variation*, *inverse variation*, or *neither*.

a. $xy = -2$ **Write original equation.**

     $y = \dfrac{}{\rule{0pt}{0pt}}$ **Divide each side by ____.**

Because $xy = -2$ _____ be written in the form $y = \dfrac{a}{x}$,

$xy = -2$ represents _____. The constant of

variation is ____.

b. $\dfrac{y}{4} = x$ **Write original equation.**

     $y = $ ____   **Multiply each side by ____.**

Because $\dfrac{y}{4} = x$ _____ be written in the form $y = ax$,

$\dfrac{y}{4} = x$ represents _____.

✓ *Checkpoint* **Tell whether the equation represents** *direct variation, inverse variation,* **or** *neither.*

1. $\dfrac{y}{-5} = x$	2. $y = 3x - 1$	3. $xy = 8$

Example 2 *Graph an inverse variation equation*

Graph $y = \dfrac{-2}{x}$.

Step 1 Make a table by choosing several integer values of x and finding the values of y. Then plot the points. To see how the function behaves for values of x very close to 0 and very far from 0, make a second table for such values and plot the points.

x	y
−4	_____
−2	_____
−1	_____
0	_____
1	_____
2	_____
4	_____

x	y
−10	_____
−5	_____
−0.5	_____
−0.2	_____
0.2	_____
0.5	_____
5	_____
10	_____

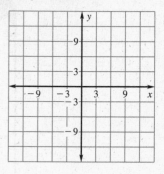

Step 2 Connect the points in Quadrant II by drawing a smooth curve through them. Repeat for points in Quadrant IV.

GRAPHS OF DIRECT VARIATION AND INVERSE VARIATION EQUATIONS

Direct Variation

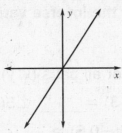

$y = ax, a > 0$

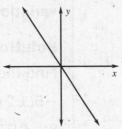

$y = ax, a < 0$

Inverse Variation

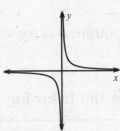

$y = \dfrac{a}{x}, a > 0$

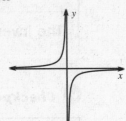

$y = \dfrac{a}{x}, a < 0$

Example 3   *Use an inverse variation equation*

The variables x and y vary inversely, and $y = -4$ when $x = 6$. Write an inverse variation equation that relates x and y. Find the value of y when $x = 3$.

Solution

Because y varies _____ with x, the equation has the form $y = \dfrac{a}{x}$. Use the fact that $x = 6$ and $y = -4$ to find the value of a.

$y = \dfrac{a}{x}$ Write inverse variation equation.

_____ $= \dfrac{a}{\boxed{}}$ Substitute ___ for x and _____ for y.

_____ $= a$ Multiply each side by ___.

An equation that relates x and y is $y = $ _____ .

When $x = 3$, $y = \dfrac{\boxed{}}{\boxed{}} = $ _____ .

Example 4   *Write an inverse variation equation*

Tell whether the ordered pairs (−5, 1.2), (−2, 3), (1.5, −4), (8, −0.75), (10, −0.6) represent inverse variation. If so, write the inverse variation equation.

Solution

Find the products xy for all pairs (x, y):

−5(1.2) = _____ , −2(3) = _____ , 1.5(−4) = _____ ,

8(−0.75) = _____ , 10(−0.6) = _____

The products are equal to the same number, _____. So,

_____ .

The inverse variation equation is $xy =$ _____ , or $y =$ _____ .

✔ *Checkpoint* **Complete the following exercises.**

4. Graph $y = \dfrac{3}{x}$.

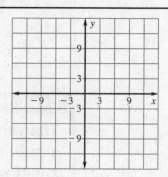

5. The variables x and y vary inversely, and $y = 5$ when $x = -3$. Write an inverse variation equation that relates x and y. Then find the value of y when $x = 9$.

Homework

6. Tell whether the ordered pairs (−20, −3), (−12, −5), (10, 6), (15, 4), (40, 1.5) represent inverse variation. If so, write the inverse variation equation.

12.2 Graph Rational Functions

Goal • Graph rational functions.

Your Notes

VOCABULARY

Rational function

PARENT RATIONAL FUNCTION

The function $y = \dfrac{1}{x}$ is the

_____ for any rational
function whose numerator has
degree 0 or 1 and whose denominator
has degree 1. The function and its
graph has the following characteristics:

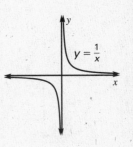

• The domain and range are all _____ real
  numbers.

• The horizontal asymptote is the ___-axis. The vertical
  asymptote is the ___-axis.

Example 1 *Compare graph of $y = \dfrac{a}{x}$ with graph of $y = \dfrac{1}{x}$*

The graph of $y = \dfrac{-1}{2x}$ is a vertical

_____ with a reflection in the

_____ of the graph of $y = \dfrac{1}{x}$.

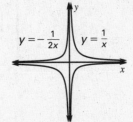

✔ *Checkpoint* **Complete the following exercise.**

1. Identify the domain and range of $y = \dfrac{1}{4x}$. Compare the graph with the graph of $y = \dfrac{1}{x}$.

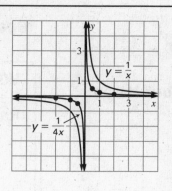

Example 2   *Graph $y = \dfrac{1}{x} + k$*

Graph $y = \dfrac{1}{x} - 2$ and identify its domain and range. Compare the graph with the graph of $y = \dfrac{1}{x}$.

Solution

Graph the function using a table of values. The domain is all real numbers except ____. The range is all real numbers except ____.

The graph of $y = \dfrac{1}{x} - 2$ is a _____ translation (of ____ units _____) of the graph of $y = \dfrac{1}{x}$.

x	y
−2	_____
−1	_____
−0.5	_____
0	_____
0.5	_____
1	_____
2	_____

✓ *Checkpoint* **Complete the following exercise.**

2. Graph $y = \dfrac{1}{x} + 2$ and identify its domain and range. Compare the graph with the graph of $y = \dfrac{1}{x}$.

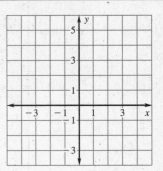

Example 3 *Graph $y = \dfrac{1}{x - h}$*

Graph $y = \dfrac{1}{x + 3}$ and identify its domain and range. Compare the graph with the graph of $y = \dfrac{1}{x}$.

Solution

Graph the function using a table of values. The domain is all real numbers except _____. The range is all real numbers except ___.

The graph of $y = \dfrac{1}{x + 3}$ is a _____ translation (of ___ units _____) of the graph of $y = \dfrac{1}{x}$.

x	y
−5	_____
−4	_____
−3.5	_____
−3	_____
−2.5	_____
−2	_____
−1	_____

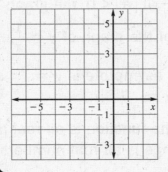

✔ *Checkpoint* **Complete the following exercise.**

3. Graph $y = \dfrac{1}{x - 1}$ and identify its domain and range. Compare the graph with the graph of $y = \dfrac{1}{x}$.

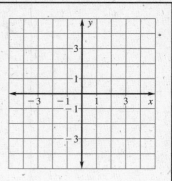

GRAPH OF $y = \dfrac{1}{x - h} + k$

The function $y = \dfrac{a}{x - h} + k$ is a _____ that has the following characteristics:

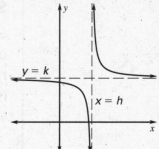

- If $|a| > 1$, the graph is a vertical _____ of the graph of $y = \dfrac{1}{x}$.

  If $0 < |a| < 1$, the graph is a vertical _____ of the graph of $y = \dfrac{1}{x}$. If $|a| < 0$, the graph is a reflection in the _____ of the graph of $y = \dfrac{1}{x}$.

- The horizontal asymptote is $y =$ ___. The vertical asymptote is $x =$ ___.

The domain of the function is all real numbers except $x =$ ___. The range is all real numbers except $y =$ ___.

Example 4   Graph $y = \dfrac{a}{x - h} + k$

Graph $y = \dfrac{2}{x - 3} + 4$.

Solution

Step 1 Identify the asymptotes of the graph. The vertical asymptote is $x =$ ___. The horizontal asymptote is $y =$ ___.

Step 2 Plot several points on each side of the _____ asymptote.

Step 3 Graph two branches that pass through the plotted points and approach the _____.

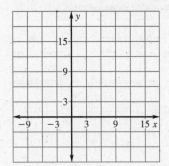

✔ **Checkpoint** Complete the following exercise.

4. Graph $y = \dfrac{3}{x + 2} - 1$.

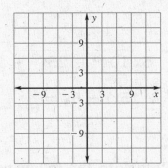

Homework

12.3 Divide Polynomials

Goal • Divide polynomials.

Example 1 *Divide a polynomial by a monomial*

Divide $10x^3 - 25x^2 + 15x$ by $5x$.

Solution

Method 1: Write the division as a fraction.

$(10x^3 - 25x^2 + 15x) \div 5x$

$$= \frac{}{}$$ **Write as a fraction.**

$$= \frac{}{} - \frac{}{} + \frac{}{}$$ **Divide each term by _____.**

$$= \underline{}$$ **Simplify.**

Method 2: Use long division.

| Think: $10x^3 \div 5x = ?$ | Think: $-25x^2 \div 5x = ?$ | Think: $15x \div 5x = ?$ |

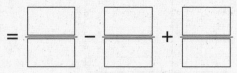

$5x \overline{)10x^3 - 25x^2 + 15x}$

$(10x^3 - 25x^2 + 15x) \div 5x = \underline{}$

To check your answer, multiply the quotient by the divisor.

✔ *Checkpoint* **Complete the following exercise.**

1. Divide $(12x^3 + 9x^2 - 3x)$ by x.

Your Notes

Example 2 *Divide a polynomial by a binomial*

Divide $4x^2 - 4x - 3$ **by** $2x + 1$.

Solution

Step 1 Divide the first term of $4x^2 - 4x - 3$ by the first term of $2x + 1$.

$$2x + 1 \overline{)4x^2 - 4x - 3}$$

Think: $4x^2 \div 2x = ?$

Multiply _____ **and** _____.

Subtract.

Step 2 Bring down _____. Then divide the first term of _____ by the first term of $2x + 1$.

$$2x + 1 \overline{)4x^2 - 4x - 3}$$

Think: $-6x \div 2x = ?$

Multiply _____ **and** _____.

Subtract.

$(4x^2 - 4x - 3) \div (2x + 1) =$ _____

Example 3 *Divide a polynomial by a binomial*

Divide $2x^2 + 9x - 6$ **by** $2x + 3$.

Solution

$$2x + 3 \overline{)2x^2 + 9x - 6}$$

Multiply ___ **and** _____.

Subtract _____. **Bring down** _____.

Multiply ___ **and** _____.

Subtract _____.

$(2x^2 + 9x - 6) \div (2x + 3) =$ _____

✓ Checkpoint **Divide.**

2. $(3x^2 - x - 14) \div (3x - 7)$

3. $(6x^2 - 13x + 11) \div (3x - 5)$

Example 4   *Rewrite polynomials*

Divide $2x + 2 + 3x^2$ by $1 + x$.

$x + 1 \overline{)3x^2 + 2x + 2}$

$\underline{}$

$\underline{}$

$\underline{}$

$\underline{}$

$(2x + 2 + 3x^2) \div (1 + x) =$ $\underline{}$

Rewrite polynomials.

Multiply ____ and _____.

Subtract _____. Bring down ___.

Multiply ____ and _____.

Subtract.

Example 5   *Insert missing terms*

Divide $-24 + 6x^2$ by $-6 + 3x$.

$3x - 6 \overline{)6x^2 + 0x - 24}$

$\underline{}$

$\underline{}$

$\underline{}$

$\underline{}$

$(-24 + 6x^2) \div (-6 + 3x) =$ $\underline{}$

Rewrite polynomials. Insert missing term.

Multiply ____ and _____.

Subtract _____. Bring down _____.

Multiply ___ and _____.

Subtract.

✔ *Checkpoint* **Divide.**

4. $(6 - 2x + x^2) \div (2 + x)$

_____

5. $(-11 + 3x^2) \div (-3 + x)$

Example 6 *Rewrite and graph a rational function*

Graph $y = \dfrac{4x - 3}{x - 1}$.

Solution

Step 1 Rewrite the rational
function in the form

$$y = \frac{a}{x - h} + k.$$

$$\begin{array}{r} \boxed{} \\ x - 1 \overline{)\, 4x - 3} \\ \underline{} \\ \end{array}$$

So, $y =$ _____ .

Step 2 Graph the function.

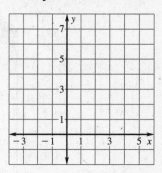

✔ *Checkpoint* **Complete the following exercise.**

6. Graph $y = \dfrac{5x + 13}{x + 3}$.

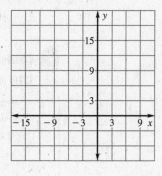

Homework

12.4 Simplify Rational Expressions

Goal • Simplify rational expressions.

Your Notes

VOCABULARY
Rational expression
Excluded value
Simplest form of a rational expression

Example 1 **Find excluded values**

Find the excluded values, if any, of the expression.

a. $\dfrac{x}{4x - 8}$

b. $\dfrac{3x}{x^2 - 16}$

Solution

a. The expression $\dfrac{x}{4x - 8}$ is undefined when

_____ $= 0$, or $x =$ ___. The excluded value is ___.

b. The expression $\dfrac{3x}{x^2 - 16}$ is undefined when

_____ $= 0$, or (_____)(_____) $= 0$.
The solutions of the equation are _____ and ___.
The excluded values are _____ and ___.

✔ **Checkpoint** Find the excluded values, if any, of the expression.

1. $\dfrac{x + 6}{14x}$	2. $\dfrac{9x + 1}{x^2 - x - 20}$

SIMPLIFYING RATIONAL EXPRESSIONS

Let a, b, and c be polynomials where $b \neq 0$ and $c \neq 0$.

Algebra

$$\frac{ac}{bc} = \frac{\boxed{}}{\boxed{}} = \underline{}$$

Example

$$\frac{3x - 9}{4x - 12} = \frac{\boxed{}}{\boxed{}} = \underline{}$$

Example 2   *Simplify expressions by dividing out monomials*

Simplify the rational expression, if possible. State the excluded values.

a. $\dfrac{18x}{6x^2} = \dfrac{\boxed{}}{\boxed{}}$ **Divide out common factors.**

$\quad = \underline{}$ **Simplify.**

The excluded value is ___.

b. $\dfrac{12x^2 - 6x}{24x} = \dfrac{\boxed{}}{\boxed{}}$ **Factor numerator and denominator.**

$\quad = \dfrac{\boxed{}}{\boxed{}}$ **Divide out common factors.**

$\quad = \dfrac{}{}$ **Simplify.**

The excluded value is ___.

✔ **Checkpoint** Simplify the rational expression, if possible. State the excluded values.

3. $\dfrac{7}{5x + 3}$	4. $\dfrac{5x}{5x^2 - 25}$	5. $\dfrac{6x^3}{2x + 4}$

Example 3   *Simplify an expression by dividing out binomials*

Simplify $\dfrac{x^2 + x - 12}{x^2 - 5x + 6}$. State the excluded values.

$\dfrac{x^2 + x - 12}{x^2 - 5x + 6} = \dfrac{\rule{3cm}{0.15mm}}{\rule{3cm}{0.15mm}}$ Factor and divide
out common factor.

$= \dfrac{}{\rule{2cm}{0.15mm}}$ Simplify.

The excluded values are ___ and ___.

Example 4   *Recognize opposites*

Simplify $\dfrac{10 + 3x - x^2}{x^2 - 25}$. State the excluded values.

$\dfrac{10 + 3x - x^2}{x^2 - 25} = \dfrac{\rule{3cm}{0.15mm}}{\rule{3cm}{0.15mm}}$ Factor numerator
and denominator.

$= \dfrac{\rule{3cm}{0.15mm}}{\rule{3cm}{0.15mm}}$ Rewrite _____
as _____.

$= \dfrac{\rule{3cm}{0.15mm}}{\rule{3cm}{0.15mm}}$ Divide out
common factor.

$= \dfrac{\rule{2cm}{0.15mm}}{\rule{2cm}{0.15mm}} = \dfrac{}{\rule{1.5cm}{0.15mm}}$ Simplify.

The excluded values are ___ and ___.

✔ *Checkpoint* Simplify the rational expression. State the excluded values.

6. $\dfrac{x^2 + 7x + 6}{x^2 + 3x - 18}$	7. $\dfrac{4 - x^2}{x^2 + 5x - 14}$

12.5 Multiply and Divide Rational Expressions

Goal • Multiply and divide rational expressions.

Your Notes

MULTIPLYING AND DIVIDING RATIONAL EXPRESSIONS

Let a, b, c, and d be polynomials.

Algebra

$$\frac{a}{b} \cdot \frac{c}{d} = \frac{\boxed{}}{\boxed{}} \text{ where } b \neq 0 \text{ and } d \neq 0$$

$$\frac{a}{b} \div \frac{c}{d} = \frac{a}{b} \cdot \frac{\boxed{}}{\boxed{}} = \frac{\boxed{}}{\boxed{}} \text{ where } b \neq 0, c \neq 0, \text{ and } d \neq 0$$

Examples

$$\frac{2x}{x + 1} \cdot \frac{x}{5} = \frac{\boxed{}}{\boxed{}} \qquad \frac{3}{x^2} \div \frac{x}{5} = \frac{3}{x^2} \cdot \frac{\boxed{}}{\boxed{}} = \frac{\boxed{}}{\boxed{}}$$

Example 1   *Multiply rational expressions involving monomials*

Find the product $\dfrac{3x^4}{4x^3} \cdot \dfrac{2x^2}{5x^3}$.

Solution

$$\frac{3x^4}{4x^3} \cdot \frac{2x^2}{5x^3} = \frac{\boxed{}}{\boxed{}}$$

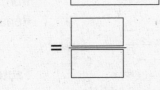 Multiply numerators and denominators.

$$= \frac{\boxed{}}{\boxed{}}$$

Product of powers property

$$= \frac{\boxed{}}{\boxed{}}$$

Factor and divide out common factors.

$$= \frac{}{}$$

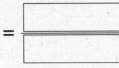 Simplify.

Example 2   *Multiply rational expressions involving polynomials*

Find the product $\dfrac{x}{5x^2 - 6x - 8} \cdot \dfrac{2x^2 - 4x}{7x^2}$.

Solution

$\dfrac{x}{5x^2 - 6x - 8} \cdot \dfrac{2x^2 - 4x}{7x^2}$

$= \overline{}$ **Multiply numerators and denominators.**

$= \overline{}$ **Factor and divide out common factors.**

$= \underline{}$ **Simplify.**

Example 3   *Multiply a rational expression by a polynomial*

Find the product $\dfrac{4x}{x^2 - x - 12} \cdot (x - 4)$.

Solution

$\dfrac{4x}{x^2 - x - 12} \cdot (x - 4)$

$= \dfrac{4x}{x^2 - x - 12} \cdot \dfrac{\boxed{}}{\boxed{}}$ **Rewrite polynomial as a fraction.**

$= \overline{}$ **Multiply numerators and denominators.**

$= \overline{}$ **Factor and divide out common factor.**

$= \underline{}$ **Simplify.**

✔ **Checkpoint** **Find the product.**

1. $\dfrac{2x^4}{5x^2} \cdot \dfrac{6x}{3x^3}$

2. $\dfrac{x^2 - 5x + 4}{3x^2 - 12x} \cdot \dfrac{2x^2 + 2}{x^2 + 6x - 7}$

3. $\dfrac{2x}{x^2 + 5x - 24} \cdot (x + 8)$

Example 4   *Divide rational expressions involving polynomials*

Find the quotient $\dfrac{x^2 + 5x - 24}{x^2 + 9x + 8} \div \dfrac{x^2 - 9}{6x - 18}.$

Solution

$\dfrac{x^2 + 5x - 24}{x^2 + 9x + 8} \div \dfrac{x^2 - 9}{6x - 18}$

$= \dfrac{x^2 + 5x - 24}{x^2 + 9x + 8} \cdot \dfrac{}{}$ **Multiply by multiplicative inverse.**

$= \dfrac{}{}$ **Multiply numerators and denominators.**

$= \dfrac{}{}$ **Factor and divide out common factors.**

$= \underline{}$ **Simplify.**

Example 5 *Divide a rational expression by a polynomial*

Find the quotient $\dfrac{x^2 - 25}{x - 3} \div (x - 5)$.

Solution

$\dfrac{x^2 - 25}{x - 3} \div (x - 5)$

$= \dfrac{x^2 - 25}{x - 3} \div \dfrac{\boxed{}}{\boxed{}}$ Rewrite polynomial as fraction.

$= \dfrac{x^2 - 25}{x - 3} \cdot \dfrac{\boxed{}}{\boxed{}}$ Multiply by multiplicative inverse.

$= \dfrac{\boxed{}}{\boxed{}}$ Multiply numerators and denominators.

$= \dfrac{\boxed{}}{\boxed{}}$ Factor and divide out common factors.

$= \dfrac{\boxed{}}{\boxed{}}$ Simplify.

✔ *Checkpoint* Find the quotient.

4. $\dfrac{x^2 + 2x - 15}{x^2 + 4x - 5} \div \dfrac{x^2 - 4}{7x - 14}$

5. $\dfrac{x^2 + 8x + 7}{x^2 - 1} \div (x + 7)$

Goal • Add and subtract rational expressions.

Your Notes

VOCABULARY

Least common denominator of rational expressions (LCD)

ADDING AND SUBTRACTING RATIONAL EXPRESSIONS WITH THE SAME DENOMINATOR

Let a, b, and c be polynomials where $c \neq 0$.

Algebra

$$\frac{a}{c} + \frac{b}{c} = \frac{\boxed{}}{\boxed{}} \qquad \frac{a}{c} - \frac{b}{c} = \frac{\boxed{}}{\boxed{}}$$

Example 1 *Add and subtract with the same denominator*

a. $\dfrac{3}{8x} + \dfrac{4}{8x} = \dfrac{\boxed{}}{8x}$ **Add numerators.**

   $= \dfrac{}{}$ **Simplify.**

b. $\dfrac{2x+9}{x+1} - \dfrac{7}{x+1} = \dfrac{\boxed{}}{x+1}$ **Subtract numerators.**

   $= \dfrac{\boxed{}}{x+1}$ **Simplify.**

   $= \dfrac{\boxed{}}{\boxed{}}$ **Factor and divide out common factor.**

   $= \underline{}$ **Simplify.**

✅ **Checkpoint** Find the sum or difference.

1. $\dfrac{x+8}{4x} + \dfrac{3}{4x}$	2. $\dfrac{6x-5}{x} - \dfrac{2x-5}{x}$

Example 2   *Find the LCD of rational expressions*

Find the LCD of the rational expressions.

a. $\dfrac{1}{3x^3}, \dfrac{5}{4x^4}$ b. $\dfrac{7}{x^2-4}, \dfrac{x+3}{x^2+x-2}$

Solution

a. Find the _____ of $3x^3$ and $4x^4$.

$3x^3 = $ _____

$4x^4 = $ _____

LCM = _____ = _____

The LCD of $\dfrac{1}{3x^3}$ and $\dfrac{5}{4x^4}$ is _____.

b. Find the _____ of x^2-4 and
x^2+x-2.

$x^2-4 = $ _____

$x^2+x-2 = $ _____

LCM = _____

The LCD of $\dfrac{7}{x^2-4}$ and $\dfrac{x+3}{x^2+x-2}$ is

_____.

✅ **Checkpoint** Find the LCD of the rational expressions.

3. $\dfrac{5}{36x}, \dfrac{x+2}{4x^3}$	4. $\dfrac{7x}{x-8}, \dfrac{x-1}{x+3}$

Example 3   *Add expressions with different denominators*

Find the sum $\dfrac{1}{3x^3} + \dfrac{5}{4x^4}$.

Solution

$\dfrac{1}{3x^3} + \dfrac{5}{4x^4}$

$= \dfrac{1 \cdot \boxed{}}{3x^3 \cdot \boxed{}} + \dfrac{5 \cdot \boxed{}}{4x^4 \cdot \boxed{}}$ **Rewrite fractions using LCD,** _____ .

$= \dfrac{\boxed{}}{\boxed{}} + \dfrac{\boxed{}}{\boxed{}}$ **Simplify numerators and denominators.**

$= \underline{}$ **Add fractions.**

Example 4   *Subtract expressions with different denominators*

Find the difference $\dfrac{x + 1}{x^2 + 5x + 6} - \dfrac{x - 4}{x^2 - 9}$.

Solution

$\dfrac{x + 1}{x^2 + 5x + 6} - \dfrac{x - 4}{x^2 - 9}$

$= \dfrac{x + 1}{(\boxed{})(\boxed{})} - \dfrac{x - 4}{(\boxed{})(\boxed{})}$

$= \dfrac{(x + 1)(\boxed{})}{\boxed{}(\boxed{})} - \dfrac{(x - 4)(\boxed{})}{\boxed{}(\boxed{})}$

$= \dfrac{\boxed{}}{\boxed{}}$

$= \dfrac{\boxed{}}{\boxed{}}$

$= \dfrac{\boxed{}}{\boxed{}}$

✔ *Checkpoint* **Find the sum or difference.**

5. $\dfrac{9}{x-1} - \dfrac{15}{3x+1}$

6. $\dfrac{12}{5x} + \dfrac{3x}{x-4}$

7. $\dfrac{x-1}{x^2-2x-24} + \dfrac{4}{x^2-5x-6}$

8. $\dfrac{x+2}{x^2+2x-15} - \dfrac{x-6}{x^2+4x-21}$

Homework

12.7 Solve Rational Equations

Goal • Solve rational equations.

Your Notes

VOCABULARY

Rational equation

Example 1 *Use the cross products property*

Solve $\dfrac{5}{x-1} = \dfrac{x}{4}$. **Check your solution.**

Solution

$\dfrac{5}{x-1} = \dfrac{x}{4}$	Write original equation.
$20 = \underline{\hspace{2cm}}$	Cross products property
$0 = \underline{\hspace{3cm}}$	Subtract _____ from each side.
$0 = (\underline{\hspace{1.5cm}})(\underline{\hspace{1.5cm}})$	Factor polynomial.
$\underline{\hspace{1.5cm}} = 0 \quad or \quad \underline{\hspace{1.5cm}} = 0$	Zero-product property
$x = \underline{\hspace{0.7cm}} \quad or \quad x = \underline{\hspace{1cm}}$	Solve for x.

The solutions are ___ and ____.

CHECK If $x =$ ___:

$$\dfrac{5}{\boxed{} - 1} \overset{?}{=} \dfrac{\boxed{}}{4}$$

$$\underline{\hspace{1cm}} = \underline{\hspace{1cm}}$$

If $x =$ ____:

$$\dfrac{5}{\boxed{} - 1} \overset{?}{=} \dfrac{\boxed{}}{4}$$

$$\underline{\hspace{1cm}} = \underline{\hspace{1cm}}$$

✔ Checkpoint Solve the equation. Check your solution.

1. $\dfrac{-2}{x+9} = \dfrac{x}{7}$	2. $\dfrac{6}{x-4} = \dfrac{3}{x}$

Example 2 *Multiply by the LCD*

Solve $\dfrac{x}{x+6} - \dfrac{1}{2} = \dfrac{4}{x+6}$.

Solution

$$\dfrac{x}{x+6} - \dfrac{1}{2} = \dfrac{4}{x+6}$$

$$\dfrac{x}{x+6} \cdot \boxed{} - \dfrac{1}{2} \cdot \boxed{} = \dfrac{4}{x+6} \cdot \boxed{}$$

$$\dfrac{\boxed{}}{x+6} - \dfrac{\boxed{}}{2} = \dfrac{\boxed{}}{x+6}$$

$$\dfrac{}{} = \underline{}$$

$$\dfrac{}{} = \underline{}$$

$$x = \underline{}$$

The solution is ____.

✔ Checkpoint Complete the following exercise.

3. Solve $\dfrac{3}{x-3} - \dfrac{1}{x+3} = \dfrac{14}{x^2-9}$. Check your solution.

Example 3 **Factor to find the LCD**

Solve $\dfrac{3}{x+2} - 1 = \dfrac{-5}{x^2 - 3x - 10}$.

Solution

Write each denominator in factored form. The LCD is

_____.

$$\dfrac{3}{x+2} - 1 = \dfrac{-5}{(x+2)(x-5)}$$

$$\dfrac{3 \cdot \boxed{}}{x+2} - 1 \cdot \boxed{}$$

$$= \dfrac{-5 \cdot \boxed{}}{(x+2)(x-5)}$$

$$\dfrac{\boxed{}}{\boxed{}} - \boxed{}$$

$$= \dfrac{\boxed{}}{\boxed{}}$$

$$\underline{} - (\underline{}) = \underline{}$$

$$\underline{} = \underline{}$$

$$\underline{} = 0$$

$$\underline{}(\underline{}) = 0$$

$$\underline{} = 0 \quad or \quad \underline{} = 0$$

$$\underline{} = \underline{}$$

$$x = \underline{} \quad or \quad x = \underline{}$$

The solutions are ___ and ___.

Homework

✓ **Checkpoint** Complete the following exercise.

4. Solve $\dfrac{1}{x+6} + 2 = \dfrac{x^2 - 38}{x^2 + 2x - 24}$

Words to Review

Give an example of the vocabulary word.

Inverse variation	Constant of variation
Hyperbola	Asymptotes of a hyperbola
Branches of a hyperbola	Rational function
Rational expression	Excluded value

Simplest form of a rational expression	Least common denominator of rational expressions
Rational equation	

Review your notes and Chapter 12 by using the Chapter Review on pages 831–834 of your textbook.

13.1 Find Probabilities and Odds

Goal • Find sample spaces and probabilities.

Your Notes

VOCABULARY

Outcome

Event

Sample space

Probability

Odds

Example 1   *Find a sample space*

You flip 2 coins. How many possible outcomes are in the sample space? List the possible outcomes.

Solution

Use a tree diagram to find the outcomes in the sample space.

Coin flip   _____   _____

Coin flip   ____ ____   ____ ____

The sample space has ___ possible outcomes. They are listed below.

_____ , _____   _____ , _____

_____ , _____   _____ , _____

✔ *Checkpoint* **Complete the following exercise.**

---

1. You flip 3 coins. How many possible outcomes are in the sample space? List the possible outcomes.

Example 2 | *Find a theoretical probability*

Marbles You reach into a bag containing 4 yellow marbles, 5 green marbles, and 6 blue marbles. What is the probability of choosing a blue marble?

Solution

There are a total of _____ = ____ marbles. So, there are ____ possible outcomes. Of all the marbles, ___ marbles are blue. There are ___ favorable outcomes.

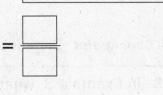

P(blue marble) = ───────────

= ───────────

= ───

= ───

✔ *Checkpoint* **Complete the following exercise.**

---

2. In Example 2, what is the probability of selecting a green marble?

Example 3 *Find the odds*

Telephone Calls A study indicates that out of every 60 telephone calls, 6 result in busy signals and 12 result in no answer. What are the odds in favor of someone answering?

Solution

There are 3 possible outcomes: _____, _____, and _____. _____ is the favorable outcome. The number of favorable outcomes is _____ = ____. _____ or _____ are unfavorable outcomes. The number of unfavorable outcomes is _____ = ____.

Odds in favor of someone answering

$$= \frac{}{}$$

$$= \frac{}{}$$

$$= \frac{}{} \quad \text{or} \quad \underline{}.$$

✓ *Checkpoint* **Complete the following exercises.**

3. In Example 3, what are the odds against someone answering?

Homework

4. In Example 3, what are the odds in favor of a busy signal?

13.2 Find Probabilities Using Permutations

Goal • Use the formula for the number of permutations.

Your Notes

VOCABULARY

Permutation _____

_____

n factorial _____

Example 1 | *Count permutations*

Consider the number of permutations of the letters in the word DOG.

a. In how many ways can you arrange all of the letters?

b. In how many ways can you arrange 2 of the letters?

Solution

a. Use the counting principle to find the number of permutations of the letters in the word DOG.

$$\begin{array}{ccccccc} \text{Number of} \\ \text{permutations} \end{array} = \begin{array}{c} \text{Choices for} \\ \text{1st letter} \end{array} \cdot \begin{array}{c} \text{Choices for} \\ \text{2nd letter} \end{array} \cdot \begin{array}{c} \text{Choices for} \\ \text{3rd letter} \end{array}$$

$$= \underline{\quad} \cdot \underline{\quad} \cdot \underline{\quad}$$

$$= \underline{\quad}$$

There are ___ ways you can arrange all of the letters.

b. When arranging 2 letters of the word DOG, you have ___ choices for the first letter and ___ choices for the second letter.

$$\begin{array}{ccccc} \text{Number of} \\ \text{permutations} \end{array} = \begin{array}{c} \text{Choices for} \\ \text{1st letter} \end{array} \cdot \begin{array}{c} \text{Choices for} \\ \text{2nd letter} \end{array}$$

$$= \underline{\quad} \cdot \underline{\quad}$$

$$= \underline{\quad}$$

There are ___ ways you can arrange 2 of the letters.

PERMUTATIONS

Formulas

The number of permutations of n objects is given by:

$$_nP_n = \underline{\quad\quad}$$

The number of permutations of n objects taken r at a time, where $r \leq n$, is given by:

$$_nP_r = \frac{\boxed{}}{\boxed{}}$$

Example 2 *Use permutations formula*

Codes A garage door has a keypad with 10 different digits. A sequence of 4 digits must be selected to open the door. How many keypad codes are possible?

Solution

To find the number of permutations of 4 digits chosen from 10, find $_{10}P_4$.

$$_{10}P_4 = \frac{10!}{(10-4)!} \qquad \text{Permutations formula}$$

$$= \frac{10!}{6!} \qquad \text{Subtract.}$$

$$= \frac{10 \cdot 9 \cdot 8 \cdot 7 \cdot 6!}{6!} \qquad \text{Expand factorials. Simplify.}$$

$$= \underline{\quad\quad} \qquad \text{Multiply.}$$

There are _____ possible keypad codes.

✓ **Checkpoint** Complete the following exercises.

1. In how many ways can you arrange the letters in the word BEAR?

2. In Example 2, suppose the code is a sequence of 5 digits. How many keypad codes are possible?

Example 3 *Find a probability using permutations*

Cards A bag contains 5 cards numbered 1–5. You draw one card at a time until you draw all 5 cards. What is the probability of drawing the card numbered 1 first and the card numbered 2 second?

Solution

Step 1 Write the number of possible outcomes as the number of permutations of the 5 cards. This is

$$\underline{}P\underline{} = \underline{}.$$

Step 2 Write the number of favorable outcomes as the number of permutations of the other cards, given that the card numbered 1 is drawn first and the card numbered 2 is drawn second. This is

$$\underline{}P\underline{} = \underline{}.$$

Step 3 Calculate the probability.

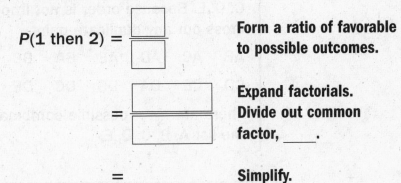

$P(1 \text{ then } 2) = \dfrac{}{}$ Form a ratio of favorable to possible outcomes.

$= \dfrac{}{}$ **Expand factorials. Divide out common factor, ____.**

$= \underline{}$ **Simplify.**

✔ **Checkpoint** Complete the following exercise.

3. In Example 3, suppose there are 10 cards in the bag numbered 1–10. Find the probability that the card numbered 1 is drawn first and the card numbered 2 is drawn second.

Homework

13.3 Find Probabilities Using Combinations

Goal • Use combinations to count possibilities.

VOCABULARY

Combination

Example 1   *Count combinations*

Count the combinations of two letters from the list A, B, C, D, E.

Solution

List all of the permutations of two letters in the list A, B, C, D, E. Because order is not important in a combination, cross out any duplicate pairs.

AB   AC   AD   AE   B̶A̶   BC   BD   BE   C̶A̶   C̶B̶

CD   CE   D̶A̶   D̶B̶   D̶C̶   DE   E̶A̶   E̶B̶   E̶C̶   E̶D̶

There are _____ possible combinations of 2 letters from the list A, B, C, D, E.

COMBINATIONS

Formula

The number of combinations of n objects taken r at a time, where $r \leq n$, is given by:

$$ {}_nC_r = \frac{\rule{3cm}{0.4pt}}{\rule{3cm}{0.4pt}} $$

Example

The number of combinations of 5 objects taken 2 at a time is:

$$ {}_5C_2 = \frac{\rule{2cm}{0.4pt}}{\rule{2cm}{0.4pt}} = \frac{\rule{2cm}{0.4pt}}{\rule{2cm}{0.4pt}} = \underline{\quad} $$

Example 2   *Use the combinations formula*

Toppings You order a pizza at a restaurant. You can choose 3 toppings from a list of 12. How many combinations of toppings are possible?

Solution

The order in which you choose the toppings is not important. So, to find the number of combinations of 12 toppings taken 3 at a time, find $_{12}C_3$.

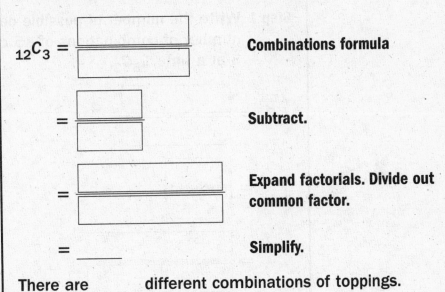

$_{12}C_3 = \dfrac{}{}$ **Combinations formula**

$= \dfrac{}{}$ **Subtract.**

$= \dfrac{}{}$ **Expand factorials. Divide out common factor.**

$= \underline{}$ **Simplify.**

There are _____ different combinations of toppings.

✓ *Checkpoint* **Complete the following exercises.**

1. Count the combinations of two letters from the list A, B, C, D, E, F.

2. In Example 2, suppose you can choose only 2 toppings out of the 12 topping choices. How many combinations are possible?

Example 3 *Find a probability using combinations*

Scholarships A committee must award three students with scholarships. Fifteen students are candidates for the scholarship including you and your two best friends. If the awardees are selected randomly, what is the probability that you and your two best friends are awarded the scholarships?

Solution

Step 1 Write the number of possible outcomes as the number of combinations of 15 candidates taken 3 at a time, $_{15}C_3$.

$$_{15}C_3 = \frac{\boxed{}}{\boxed{}}$$

$$= \frac{\boxed{}}{\boxed{}}$$

$$= \frac{\boxed{}}{\boxed{}}$$

$$= \underline{}$$

Step 2 Find the number of favorable outcomes. Only _____ of the possible combinations includes scholarships for you and your two best friends.

Step 3 Calculate the probability.

P(scholarships awarded to you and your friends) =

_____

☑ *Checkpoint* **Complete the following exercise.**

Homework

3. In Example 3, suppose there are 20 candidates for the scholarships. Find the probability that you and your two best friends are awarded the 3 scholarships.

13.4 Find Probabilities of Compound Events

Goal • Find the probability of a compound event.

Your Notes

VOCABULARY

Compound event
_____

Mutually exclusive events
_____

Overlapping events
_____

Independent events
_____

Dependent events
_____

Example 1   *Find the probability of A or B*

You roll a number cube. Find the probability that you roll a 4 or a prime number.

Solution

Because 4 is not a prime number, rolling a 4 and rolling a prime number are _____ events.

$P(4 \text{ or prime}) = $ _____ + _____

$\qquad\qquad = \dfrac{\;\;}{\;\;} + \dfrac{\;\;}{\;\;}$

$\qquad\qquad = \dfrac{\;\;}{\;\;}$

$\qquad\qquad = \dfrac{\;\;}{\;\;}$

Your Notes

Example 2 *Find the probability of A or B*

You roll a number cube. Find the probability that you roll an even number or a number greater than 3.

Solution

Because ___ and ___ are both even and greater than 3, rolling an even number and rolling a number greater than three are _____ events. There are ___ even numbers, ___ numbers greater than 3, and ___ numbers that are both.

$P(\text{even or} > 3)$

= _____ + _____ – _____

= ___ + ___ – ___

= ___

= ___

✔ *Checkpoint* **Complete the following exercises.**

1. You roll a number cube. Find the probability that you roll a 1 or a 6.

2. You roll a number cube. Find the probability that you roll an even number or a 2.

Example 3   *Find the probability of A and B*

You roll two number cubes. What is the probability that you roll a 1 first and a 2 second?

Solution

The events are _____. The number on one number cube does not affect the other.

$P(1 \text{ and } 2) = \underline{\hspace{1cm}} \cdot \underline{\hspace{1cm}} = \underline{\hspace{1cm}} \cdot \underline{\hspace{1cm}} = \underline{\hspace{1cm}}$

Example 4   *Find the probability of A and B*

Miniature Golf You and a friend must each select a golf ball from a bucket to play miniature golf. There are 3 yellow balls, 4 red balls, 5 green balls, and 4 purple balls. You select a golf ball and then your friend selects a golf ball. What is the probability that both golf balls are green?

Solution

Because you do not replace the first ball, the events are _____. Before you choose a ball, there are ____ balls and ____ are green. After you choose a green ball, there are ____ balls and ____ are green.

$P(\text{green } and \text{ then green})$

$= \underline{\hspace{2cm}} \cdot \underline{\hspace{3cm}}$

$= \underline{\hspace{1cm}} \cdot \underline{\hspace{1cm}} = \underline{\hspace{1cm}} = \underline{\hspace{1cm}}$

✓ **Checkpoint** Complete the following exercise.

3. A bag contains 6 red marbles, 5 green marbles, and 3 blue marbles. You randomly draw 2 marbles, one at a time. Find the probability that both are red if:

   a. you replace the first marble.

   b. you do not replace the first marble.

13.5 Analyze Surveys and Samples

Goal • Identify populations and sampling methods.

VOCABULARY

Survey

_____

Population

_____

Sample

_____

Biased sample

_____

Biased question

SAMPLING METHODS

In a _____ sample, every member of the population has an equal chance of being selected.

In a _____ sample, the population is divided into distinct groups. Members are selected at random from each group.

In a _____ sample, a rule is used to select members of the population.

In a _____ sample, only members of the population who are easily accessible are selected.

In a _____ sample, members of the population select themselves by volunteering.

Example 1   *Classify a sampling method*

Study Time A high school is conducting a survey to determine the average number of hours that their students spend doing homework each week. At the school, only the members of the sophomore class are chosen to complete the survey. Identify the population and classify the sampling method.

Solution

The population is _____. Because a rule (sophomore class only) is used to select members of the population, the sample is a _____ sample.

Example 2   *Identify a potentially biased sample*

Is the sampling method used in Example 1 likely to result in a biased sample?

Solution

Students in other grades may have different study habits, so the method _____ in a biased sample.

Example 3   *Identify potentially biased questions*

Tell whether the question is potentially biased. Explain your answer. If the question is potentially biased, rewrite it so that it is not.

a. Do you still support the school basketball team, even though the team is having its worst season in 5 years?

b. Don't you think that dogs are better pets than cats?

Solution

a. This question is biased because _____

_____

_____. An unbiased question is,

" _____ "

b. This question is biased because _____

_____. An unbiased question is

" _____ "

    Lesson 13.5 • **Algebra 1 Notetaking Guide**   **309**

✅ *Checkpoint* **Complete the following exercises.**

1. In Example 1, suppose the school asks students to volunteer to take the survey. Classify the sampling method.

---

2. **Amusement Park** An amusement park owner wants to evaluate the customer service given by the park's ride operators. One day, every 10th customer leaving the park was asked, "Don't you think that our friendly, well-trained ride operators provided excellent customer service today?"

   a. Is this sampling method likely to result in a biased sample? Explain.

   b. Is this question potentially biased? Explain your answer. If the question is potentially biased, rewrite it so that it is not.

Homework

13.6 Use Measures of Central Tendency and Dispersion

Goal • Compare measures of central tendency and dispersion.

Your Notes

VOCABULARY

Measure of dispersion

Range

Mean absolute deviation

MEASURES OF CENTRAL TENDENCY

The _____, or *average*, of a numerical data set is denoted by $\bar{x}$, which is read as "x-bar." For the data set $x_1, x_2, \ldots, x_n$, the mean is

$$\bar{x} = \frac{\boxed{}}{\boxed{}}.$$

The _____ of a numerical data set is the _____ _____ when the numbers are written in numerical order. If the data set has an even number of values, the median is the _____.

The _____ of a data set is the value that _____ _____. There may be one mode, no mode, or more than one mode.

Example 1 *Compare measures of central tendency*

Test Scores Your last 8 test scores are listed below. Find the mean, median, and mode(s) of the data.

81   87   91   91   93   95   98   100

Solution

$$\bar{x} = \dfrac{\boxed{}}{\boxed{}}$$

$$= \dfrac{\boxed{}}{\boxed{}} = \underline{}$$

The median is the mean of the two middle values, _____ and _____, or _____.

The mode is _____.

✓ **Checkpoint** Complete the following exercise.

1. Find the mean, median, and mode(s) of the data set.

13, 15, 15, 19, 23, 26, 27, 30

MEASURES OF DISPERSION

The _____ of a numerical data set is the difference of the greatest value and the least value.

The _____ of the data set $x_1, x_2, \ldots, x_n$, is given by:

$$\boxed{}$$

Example 2 *Compare measures of dispersion*

Golf The 9-hole scores of golfers on two different high school teams are given. Compare the spread of the data sets using (a) the range and (b) the mean absolute deviation.

Team 1: 51, 46, 40, 49, 55, 47

Team 2: 41, 47, 54, 50, 42, 42

Solution

a. Team 1: _____   Team 2: _____

The range of set 1 is _____ the range of set 2. So, the data in _____ cover a wider interval than the data in _____.

b. The mean of set 1 is _____, so the mean absolute deviation is:

$$\frac{\rule{8cm}{0pt}}{\rule{8cm}{0pt}} = \rule{1.5cm}{0pt}.$$

The mean of set 2 is _____, so the mean absolute deviation is:

$$\frac{\rule{8cm}{0pt}}{\rule{8cm}{0pt}} = \rule{1.5cm}{0pt}.$$

The mean absolute deviation of _____ is greater, so the average variation from the mean is greater for the data in _____ than for the data in _____.

✓ **Checkpoint** Complete the following exercise.

2. **Golf** The 9-hole scores of golfers on Team 3 are 43, 52, 46, 44, 42, and 43. Compare the spread of the data with that of set 2 in Example 2 using (a) the range and (b) the mean absolute deviation.

13.7 Interpret Stem-and-Leaf Plots and Histograms

Goal • Make stem-and-leaf plots and histograms.

Your Notes

> ## VOCABULARY
>
> Stem-and-leaf plot
> _____
>
> Frequency
> _____
>
> Frequency table
> _____
>
> Histogram

Example 1 *Make a stem-and-leaf plot*

Survey A survey asked people how many miles they commute to work. The results are listed below. Make a stem-and-leaf plot of the data.

5, 10, 18, 15, 9, 27, 10, 35, 12, 4, 8, 14, 23, 2, 20, 5, 15

Solution

Step 1 Separate the data into stems and leaves.

Step 2 Write the leaves in _____.

Miles

Stem	Leaves
0	_____
1	_____
2	_____
3	_____

Miles

Stem	Leaves
0	_____
1	_____
2	_____
3	_____

Key: 3 | 5 = _____

✔ **Checkpoint** Complete the following exercise.

1. Make a stem-and-leaf plot of the data.

3.4, 4.3, 5.9, 6.2, 5.3, 3.7, 3.9, 4.7, 3, 4.8, 6.3, 3.6, 3.2, 3.4

Example 2 *Interpret a stem-and-leaf plot*

Fundraiser Sales The back-to-back stem-and-leaf plot shows the fundraiser sales (in hundreds of dollars) of the homerooms of two different grades. Compare the sales of each grade.

Fundraiser Sales

9th Grade   10th Grade

```
          5 | 5 |
        7 5 | 6 | 6 8 9
      7 4 3 | 7 | 0 2 5 5 7 9
  6 5 3 3 1 | 8 | 3
```

Key: 3 | 7 | 0 = 7.3, 7.0

Solution

Consider the distribution of the data. The interval for 7.0 and 7.9 hundreds of dollars in sales contains _____ of the 10th grade homerooms, while the interval for 8.0 and 8.9 hundreds of dollars in sales contains _____

_____. The clustering of the data shows that the _____ fundraiser sales were generally higher than the _____ fundraiser sales.

Example 3 *Making a histogram*

Birth Weight The birth weight (in ounces) of babies born at a hospital are listed below. Make a histogram of the data.

96, 128, 115, 120, 107, 125, 136, 122, 131, 112, 110

Solution

Step 1 Choose intervals of _____ size that cover all of the data values. Organize the data using a

_____.

Step 2 Draw the bars of the histogram using the intervals from the frequency table.

Birth weight	Babies
90–99	
100–109	
110–119	
120–129	
130–139	

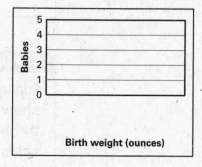

Birth weight (ounces)

✔ *Checkpoint* **Complete the following exercise.**

2. Make a histogram of the data.

   19.00, 18.59, 19.80, 20.52, 18.73, 20.89, 20.12, 18.17, 20.62

Homework

13.8 Interpret Box-and-Whisker Plots

Goal • Make and interpret box-and-whisker plots.

Your Notes

VOCABULARY

Box-and-whisker plot

Quartile

Interquartile range

Outlier

Example 1 *Make a box-and-whisker plot*

Height Make a box-and-whisker plot of the heights (in inches) of 7 family members: 34, 67, 70, 62, 46, 75, 54.

Step 1 Order the data. Then find the median and quartiles.

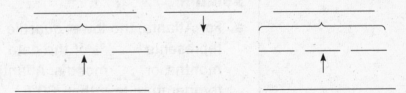

Step 2 Plot the median, the quartiles, the maximum value, and the minimum value below a number line.

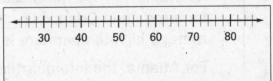

Step 3 Draw a _____ from the lower quartile to the upper quartile. Draw a vertical line through the _____. Draw a line segment from the box to the maximum and another from the box to the minumum.

✓ Checkpoint **Complete the following exercise.**

> **1.** Make a box-and-whisker plot of the data.
>
> 10, 8, 2, 4, 3, 8, 6, 4, 5, 5

Example 2 *Interpret a box-and-whisker plot*

Average Temperature The box-and-whisker plots below show the average high temperature (in degrees Fahrenheit) each month in Atlanta, Georgia and Orlando, Florida.

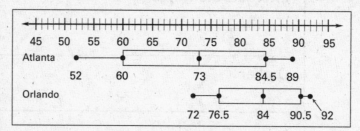

a. For how many months is Atlanta's average high temperature less than 60°F?

b. Compare the average high temperature in Atlanta with the average high temperature in Orlando.

Solution

a. For Atlanta, the lower quartile is ____. A whisker represents ____% of the data, so for ____% of ____ months, or ____ months, Atlanta has an average high temperature less than 60°F.

b. The median average high temperature for a month in Atlanta is _____. The median average high temperature for a month in Orlando is _____. In general, the average high temperature is _____ in Orlando.

For Atlanta, the interquartile range is _____, or _____ °F. For Orlando, the interquartile range is _____, or ____ °F. The range for Atlanta is _____ than the range for Orlando. So, Atlanta has _____ variation in average high temperature per month.

✓ **Checkpoint** **Complete the following exercise.**

> **2.** In Example 2, for how many months was the average high temperature in Orlando more than 84°F?

Example 3   *Identify an outlier*

The average monthly high temperatures (in degrees Fahrenheit) in Atlanta are: 52, 57, 65, 73, 80, 87, 89, 88, 82, 73, 63, 55. These data were used to create the box-and-whisker plot in Example 2. Find the outlier(s) of the data set, if possible.

Solution

From Example 2, you know the interquartile range of the data is _____°F. Find 1.5 times the interquartile range: 1.5(_____) = _____.

From Example 2, you also know that the lower quartile is _____ and the upper quartile is _____. A value less than _____ – _____ = _____ is an outlier. A value greater than _____ + _____ = _____ is an outlier.

Because there is _____ value less than _____ and there is _____ value greater than _____, this data set _____ an outlier.

✓ **Checkpoint** **Complete the following exercise.**

> **3.** Find the outlier(s) of the data set, if possible.
>
> 22, 29, 15, 25, 9, 32, 49, 20, 33, 26, 19, 30

Homework

Words to Review

Give an example of the vocabulary word.

Outcome	Event
Sample space	Probability
Odds	Permutation
n factorial	Combination
Compound event	Mutually exclusive events

Overlapping events	Independent events
Dependent events	**Survey**
Population	**Sample**
Biased sample	**Biased question**

Measure of dispersion	Range
Mean absolute deviation	Stem-and-leaf plot
Frequency	Frequency table
Histogram	Quartile

Interquartile range	Outlier
Box-and-whisker plot	

Review your notes and Chapter 13 by using the Chapter Review on pages 896–900 of your textbook.